3P'S - PLEASURE, PAIN, & PASSION

GREGORY C. WHITESIDE JR.

Condemned Row

CONTENTS

DEDICATION

This Poetry Book is dedicated to my Whole Family, All of my wonderful Friends, and especially to Our Heavenly Father ABOVE ALL ELSE!!! With a special thanks to my Mother "Flora B.", my Grandmother "Catherine L.", My sister "Shirley C.", my nephew "Tyrone C.", my nieces (The Twins) Natasha "Sexy Chocolate" C. & Nachole "Chicken" C , BIG Bill & Brooke "Cookie" M. & The Whole M/R Clan, Andrel "DRE" T., my Pop's Wayne "BIG WEEZ B., Gamal "Strainj" N., and Demean "CHAMP" B.,...All of you have touched my life in a special way and without your love, support and inspiration this book could have never come into existence...And to the BIG HOMIE "RU-AL" thank you for giving me the blueprints to make this book come together... YOU ARE ALL VERY MUCH APPRECIATED!!!

LOVE WITHOUT A LIMIT,
YOUR HUMBLE BROTHER,
Gregory C. Whiteside Jr.
A.K.A. : G-BONE

INTRODUCTION

BOOK CREATOR - Gregory C. Whiteside Jr. a.k.a: G-BONE

First of all I want to send much love and respect to you and all of your loved ones. Thank you for all of your love and support and for purchasing this book...**YOU ARE APPRECIATED!!!**

Well I'm a Death Row Inmate at San Quentin State Prison and I wrote this poetry book in hopes to share with the world all of the different aspects of my life and all the love, pain, joy & sorrow that's within my heart. I hope to inspire people with how I've expressed myself in these poems and show them that we all go through changes in life and they are not alone in their pain and struggles; as well as their joy and love. I use my poetry as therapy to express how I'm feeling and to help me get through both the tough times and to remember the good times; and though I'm on Death Row I pray that when you read this book you will have a glimpse into my heart, my mind and my soul; and though my life may end my spirit can never be extinguished...Enjoy this book and know that the

love in my heart is without a limit...PEACE TO YOU
ALWAYS...

G -BONE

"WAITING TO DIE - (PART #1)"

Growing up from place to place

Never knew my father, mother's on freebase

She started off by smoking weed

But then it turned to crack, heroin & speed (DAMN!!!)

Everyday there was debate

With no food on my plate...Denied Section 8

What kind of life for me was this

Seeing people rich and we ain't got sh*t

Growing up I learned to hate

Quick to criticize people for old mistakes

They might have made in the past

Until I got a wake up call with a foot in my a**

Mom threw me out the house

And said I'll never be sh*t running off at the mouth

Now what am I to do

The homie called up and said G-BONE I thought you knew

You could call me at any time

Because I'm down to die for yours and you're down to die for mine

To survive we did crime

Hung out with the thugs thinking everything would be fine

But ended up doing time

And being locked up plays tricks on your mind

Not know if it's night or day

In a cell with men 300 pounds and GAY!!!

Now I can stand here on Death Row and say I'm ready to die today!!!

I'M WAITING TO DIE!!!

"WAITING TO DIE - (PART #2)"

I've got more LOVE in my heart than Donald Trump's got
dollars

But I grew up in poverty at the damn Watt's Tower

My mom's on the county and I'm searching for a dollar

My life's full of pain every minute, every hour

We go through life in search of peace

But I can't even find peace when I sleep

I toss and turn when I think of life

Because I'm living in darkness in search of light

I just can't stand everyday not knowing

In which direction my life is going

Because everybody else wants to be a part of something

But a brother like me just want to be a part of nothing

Because I'm in pain...More pain than "Tupac"

Not having the things that a poor man got

I tried to rob but ended up getting shot

And all I remember is the sound of the glock

Now I got medical bills and where are my friends

The bills pile up and ain't nobody pitching in

So what to do, will the doctors let me die

My family is poor so all they can do is cry

Now my pulse is weak and my temperature's dropping

I'm ready to die so can somebody do something

They said yeah, go ahead and pull the plug

Pull out the scalpel, put on the rubber gloves I had no money so nobody showed love

So I float away to the land of above... No longer Waiting To Die...

"CAN YOU FORGIVE ME???" (THE PRAYER)

Now that I sit here confined
A lot of things that I did wrong come to mind
Too busy with the ways of the world to see the warning signs
Too selfish and cold—hearted to lend a helping hand or
be kind
Never had the time because my feelings changed like the
weather
So If you asked me how many times I helped a stranger , I'd
have to say never
And if you asked me how many times I've prayed for my
enemies, I'd say not ever
And if you asked me how many times I've sinned, I couldn't
count them all together
And I know I've done everything to offend Thee
Can you forgive?? Can You Forgive Me???

Baby...This apology is for every time I did you wrong
For every time you had to sit at home alone because I was in
the streets gone

For all my selfish inconsiderations
For all the times you had to put up with my rude impatience
For every time I disrespected you in private and in public
For every time I hurt your feelings and told you to just shove it
I was young and stupid thinking I was the life of the party
And in the process I hurt the only one who ever really loved me...BABY I'M SO SORRY!!!
And I know I've done everything to offend Thee
Can you forgive?? Can You Forgive Me???

I've lied, I've cheated, I've stole, I've held a grudge
I've hated, I've debated, instead of a hug I gave a shove
The many problems I've created have left many devastated
And that goes for my family and many others unrelated
HOW COULD I BE SO DAMN INSINCERE??!!
I've pushed everyone away then wonder why they're not here
Because I've done so wrong for so long and did it with all my power
And I'm so ashamed because I know You saw it all Heavenly Father
And I know I've done everything to offend Thee
Can you forgive?? Can You Forgive Me???

I've crippled the weak and trampled the poor
I've held on the wrath and knocked on Death's door
If only I knew then what sin finally had in store
I've stumbled through life not even knowing what to live for
Now I meditate on Your Word in hopes of changing my eternal fate
I repent and praise You everyday hoping it's not too little too late
And I know nothing is too hard for you to create

I live for You so I hope You can create forgiveness for me,
Your servant's sake
And I know I've done everything to offend Thee
PLEASE!!! Can you forgive?? CAN YOU FORGIVE ME???

"PROVERBS OF EMOTIONS"

Infidelity is a heartbreaker - Death is a life taker

Loneliness is a forsaker - Tragedy is a soul shaker

Despair is dark, Revenge is darker

Hate is easy, but maintaining Love is harder

Joy is abundant in the laughter of a child

But wrath is an uncontrollable fire when left to run wild

Peace is what everyone longs for

But an unhealing wound is always the ending result of
any War

Laziness brings poverty to all who seek her

But Betrayal is always a pain that hurts deeper

Wisdom is the key to success and all knowledge

But foolishness is the path to failure and all garbage

Greed is a motivator but it's owner is left empty and unsatisfied

Evil is a plague that utterly annihilates all who let him inside

Misery leaves all who entertain her feeling useless

Pride is stubborn and you're destined to fall if you abuse this

Self Esteem is inconsistent, sometimes up sometimes down

But none can survive when Anger & Jealousy come to town

A Phony goes hand and hand with a fraud and a fake

Selfishness will do anything to get ahead no matter what it takes

Beauty is in the eye of the beholder, but at some point we all meet Lust

Honesty is so honorable, I mean who else are you going to trust

Sorrow will have your eyes filled with tears

But Courage will help you defeat all your fears

With Happiness Harmony is received

And with Faith all will believe

Because there is a sea of feelings as vast as the oceans

So tell me how you feel about my Proverbs Of Emotions...

"COMPLETE"

Just like candy You are so sweet
With a smile so beautiful and so unique
You bring Peace & Harmony with no need to compete
But at the same time Your Love could never be beat
You have such elegant style & grace from your head to
your feet
And total Bliss is what I feel whenever we meet
Every moment with You is such a treat
My passion burns for You...Can't You feel the heat???
So I want You to know my Love for You is as solid as concrete
Because You fill me with joy - You Make Me Complete...

"MUTUAL"

Somebody please tell me what to do

Because the sun shines brighter when I'm next to you

I can't keep my mind off sexing you

When I think about being next to you

But I'm just too shy to let you know

But somehow I've got to let my feelings show

Infatuation turns to LOVE if you let it grow

But only if the feelings are MUTUAL...

"THAT'S WHY I LOVE YOU"

When I was riding high You were there to fly with me
When I was feeling low You were there to cry with me
When I was going through Hell You went through the flames
with me
And when "Death" came You were even willing to die
with me
That's Why I Love You...

Nothing can compare to the love that we share
From the moment we met it's always been there
I never knew love like this with such tender loving care
Your love runs so deep that it's almost more than I can bear
That's Why I Love You...

When we're together joy is the product we create
And when we're united bliss is the product that we make
And when we kiss it's like a bomb that we detonate
Because "REAL LOVE" is explosive and can not be faked
That's Why I Love You...

Your love always has my back
Your love makes sure I never lack
Your love never slacks
Because only within your love can I live life to the max
That's Why I Love You...

Your love is a light that shines on me everyday
It lights the path to Heaven's Doorway
The love You give me is priceless so how could I ever
repay???
And you've seen me at my worst but still love me anyway
THAT'S WHY I LOVE!!!

"YOU ARE LOVED"

Beauty, Style, Grace
Beautiful hips, beautiful face
Can I have a taste???
Make haste to feel the enormity of my sexual ardor
You're everything I'm asking for, but OH SO MUCH MORE!!!

You illuminate my mind's eye
But most can't see pass what's between your thighs
As for I, I want to know what's between your ears,
and what's behind your big beautiful eyes...
What secrets do they hold?? What stories left untold???
You're worth more than diamonds, platinum & gold...

My soul yearns to be one with yours
But for right now that may be too much to ask for
I want you totally and completely - Mind, Body and Soul -
The good & bad - The Ying & Yang...
Now I understand why "Marvin Gaye" sang : "Distant
Lover...Come To Me..."

Do you feel the awesome power of my feelings for you???
I just want to love you, to kiss and hug you, and only put
God above you...

You are the best, the undisputed most beautiful woman in the
world!!!
That's factual and actual
You're a real woman and not a little girl,
That's why I took this time to ask you...Will you be mine???
YOU ARE LOVED...

"MY INSPIRATION"

Girl your body's like dynamite
And I have to admit that I kinda like
The way your body sways from side to side
So come with me if you're down to ride...

Because I was alone until you came into my life
And you never knew I would cry myself to sleep every night
Now I have hopes of making you my wife
Because my love for you is deep like the sacrifice of Christ...

Still I pray everyday hoping you won't go away
And I love you with everything I am hoping it will make
you stay
Because your love is priceless so how can I ever afford to pay
And there are no words to truly describe your beauty, so
what can I say???

Your presence instantly puts me in the mood for romance
We've all loved and lost but for you I'd take a chance

Because you're always beautiful but your smile makes your
beauty enhance
And every time you come around my heart seems to flutter
and dance...

And it's a shame because you don't even realize how special
you are
I know with you by my side we can go far
Because in the past I've been hurt and on my heart there was
a scar
But you healed my broken heart because you are my lucky
star...

So give me your love - Don't keep me waitin'
Because I can say that I truly love you without hesitation
You are the product of "True Love's" manifestation You're my
reason for living - You're My Inspiration...

"ABANDONED BY HOPE"

If you've been where I'm at if you've seen what I see -

Then you'll know I'm going thru HELL

a place where even HOPE has abandoned me -

The storms of my life

haven't let up yet -

So my life's filled with painful memories and nightmares that I can never forget -

The Devil has sent his demons

to attack me and not relent -

I may bend but I refuse to break

though my spirit is spent -

Is it blasphemy

for you to blast for me -

And shoot down these damn demons

who have been attacking me -

For me it's been rough

but the pain is getting worse -

"GOD" always wanted to bless me

but I disobeyed Him and reaped a curse -

On Earth it's a prison cell

for those who sin & rebel -

Doomed are most who enter here for this is a living HELL -

For me it might be too late

but hopefully it's not for you -

So take heed to these words of wisdom

DO GOOD WHENEVER POSSIBLE AND LET "GOD" USE YOU!!! -

Otherwise you'll be where I'm at

you'll see what I see -

You'll be going thru the same HELL too

A PLACE WHERE EVEN HOPE WILL ABANDON THEE...

"THE PAIN IS GETTING WORSE"

I've been a liar, a thief, a hoodlum, a thug
I've held on to pain, I've held on to grudge
I've never known peace,
I've never felt love
And my stupid pride causes me to push & shove
You away from me, because ain't no saving me
My pain is so deep that Death can't take it away from me
And what's worse is I've been cursed, from my birth to the
hearse
I never thought it'd get this bad, but the pain is getting worse
The Pain Is Getting Worse...

I've been beat down, broken, torn & used
I've been kicked, punched, pummeled & abused
It's left me confused, so I rack my brain
And without any real answers, I've gone quite insane
Because I'm trapped in a world with the off-spring of "Cain"
No escaping these chains, no sunshine - only rain

And what's worse is I've been cursed, trapped inside Satan's turf
I never thought it'd get this bad, but the pain is getting worse
The Pain Is Getting Worse...

I've been lied to, bamboozled, hoodwinked, cheated
I'm left undone with all my efforts defeated
I can't beat it...The pain is taking over (Ovah)
Because the one's that I trusted now act like they don't know ya
So what's left to do, but just curse God and die
But it's not in me to give up, so while I'm alive I'm going to try
To do the best I can even though I've been cursed
Because I can take the pain, though the pain is getting worse
THE PAIN IS GETTING WORSE!!!

Epilogue: *"Oh wretched man that I am!! Who shall deliver me from this body of Death??!!"*
-Romans 7:24-

"TODAY IS THE BIRTHPLACE OF FOREVER"

Today is the birthplace of forever

The progression of time none can sever

With each passing second we struggle with the secrets of the heart & mind

But all will be revealed through the passage of time

And as the sands in the hourglass fall

We get closer to understanding it all

Time must not be wasted -

Life gives our spirit the potential to bloom

We must learn from yesterday, grow today, hoping tomorrow will be here soon

But what is tomorrow because in reality we can only live in today

Tomorrow has never been promised, but for a bright future is what we all pray

In this world of woe most are so tired and hoping today will end

But as time keeps slipping into the future today continues to transcend

This time thing, how does it work?? Will we always be in a state of today???

Only The Creator knows...Only He can show us the way

I tell you "Today" is on such a higher level

It's like trying to understand Heaven & Hell or God & The Devil

With the Moon & Sun, Darkness & Light, Night & Day

The path of Today will never end or stray

Fools say I'll see you tomorrow because surely tomorrow will come eventually

But then they died moments later not knowing tomorrow they will never see

So stop stressing about tomorrow and live for Today because in reality

It's always Today and tomorrow is not promised to you or me

And the progression of time none can sever

Because Today Is The Birthday Of Forever...

"LOVED AND LOST"

Do you know how it feels to have loved and lost
With your emotions in turmoil, turned and tossed
I've paid the price at an unspeakable cost
I see my heart's turned cold, I'm looking at the frost...

I loved you when no one else would
I gave you my all - The best that I could
And I defended you when others said you were no good
But you did me so wrong that no amount of love could have
withstood...

You enchanted me with your smile
And I loved the way your hair laid across your brow
But you changed so dramatically after a while
And turned a love so beautiful into something so foul...

At first it was kisses, hugs & back rubs
At the end it was fussing, fighting, pushes & shoves Instead
of beautiful smiles all I got was mean mugs

And those are the things that no one could love...

With tenderness and humility to you I stayed loyal
But you lied and cheated and made my temperature boil
All my hopes and dreams for us you always seemed to foil
You're like a python strangling me within your coil...

But I still tried to love you even after all that
Even after you walked all over me like a doormat
Because I didn't want to believe the absolute fact
That you were truly evil with a heart that was black...

Now I've paid the price at an unspeakable cost
And my heart's turned cold, I'm looking at the frost
Because my emotions are in turmoil, turned & tossed
But now I know how it feels to have Loved And Lost...

"OXYMORON"

I never be fallin', but I'm always trippin'

And I'm always failin', but still complete my mission...

And in addition I can't add, I take away but can't subtract

I speak the truth but not the facts, I start in first but end up last...

I'm unbroken but in a cast, I see the future but not the past

I'm dynamite but scared to blast, I'm slow to argue but whip a** fast...

I love freedom but I'm locked behind steel,

I'm in a world of phonies but my reality ain't even real -

If we all love life then why do so many kill,

I'm so emotional but I don't know how to feel...

I love everyone but hate them just the same,

Because my sweetest joy causes me the most pain -

GOD gave us the freedom of choice but at the same time it's a chain,

We all sin the same, can our nature ever change???

The caged bird sings even though it's locked up,

And if you ask anyone,"Where did GOD come from?",They'll probably say,"What?!"

I love when it rains but thunder & lightening are so frightening,

Why in the name of PEACE do people do so much fighting -

I guess it's cruel kindness - It's like true lying,

Because you don't know how to live until you're already dying...

A picture says a thousand words, but it never speaks,

Beautiful but she turns ugly if her attitude stinks...

The pursuit of sweet honey turns sour if stung by a bee,

I think you have to go blind before you truly can see...

You can be rich in cash but poor in spirit,

Everyone's screaming for love but no one seems to hear it...

Many succeed through failure - You can't break through without a barrier,

Most that are humble are superior - True strength comes from the wearier...

What feels so right can be so wrong,

A gun can save a life but also make one gone -

What makes you cry can turn into a love song,

Is Death really the end or will life eternally carry on???

I'm G-BONE and one day my life will end, but my words will forever go on -

Contradiction - Paradox...Life's the ultimate OXYMORON...

"WITHOUT YOU"

My body's the Earth, my tears are the rain
My spirit is the wind, but without you I'm in pain

I own the heavens above to the Earth's core that burns
beneath
But life without you is meaningless and incomplete

I'm the Sun too, and my sunshine is my smile I give you in
full brilliance
But there's no other in creation with your significance or
magnificence

You're the key that opens the door to a majestic house & land
But without you the house has no foundation and the land
turns into quicksand

I'm the birds that soar and sings nature's beautiful song
But my wings have been clipped and I have no reason to sing
with you gone

I'm a busy bee humming and my nectar is the honey you
bring
But if my honey has been taken away people watch out for
my bitter sting

I'm the ocean and you're the most beautiful fish in my sea
But without you pollution has overtaken me

I'm a comet traveling through galaxies throughout the
universe
But without your loving telescope no one will see me from
planet Earth

I'm a shooting star falling from far beyond
But without you I may never be wished upon

I'm a roaring lion and of all beast I'm the king
But this vast kingdom means nothing without you my Queen

I have a 200 I.Q. and scientist say I'm a genius without doubt
But how someone can live without you I could never
figure out

Life's a puzzle - That's hard to figure out - To say the least
But I've found the answer - It lies within you - You're the
missing piece

Now life seems so real, so clear, so true
But I could have never solved this puzzle...WITHOUT YOU!!!

"WITHOUT YOU - (REVAMPED)"

Your smile was like a rainbow in the sky
It was so beautiful it would make me cry
But it was tear of joy in my eyes
And my love for you was the reason why...

But it's been lonely days & sleepless nights
Every since you've been out of my life
I'm in pain at this moment as I write
And filled with a dread & anguish I just can't fight...

Now I'm torn & shattered because your love was the glue
That held me together and made me brand new
So now what am I supposed to do
Because my life will never be complete...Without you...

"LONELY"

When I get lonely
I think of you only
And those thoughts console me
I just wish you could hold me...

Because all I want is you
Truly wonderful in all you do
I'm so lonely without you
But it seems you never knew...

Now on this desolate road to tomorrow
I sit alone to wallow in my sorrow
My heart beats but it feels so hollow
In my longing for affection am I being selfish & shallow???

It's like I'm a lone wolf in a wilderness land
Like Adam before Eve, just a lonely man
With the cards I was dealt I'm doing the best I can But until
you've been lonely you won't understand...

And I've tried to be patient, waiting for Love's return
But without you I'm lonely, and my passionate fire ceases
to burn
How to go on without you I still haven't learned
Does anyone care?? Is anyone concerned???

I miss your love, it ment the world to me
But now I'm alone and think of only Thee
And when I sleep I dream of you only
Hoping you don't feel like I do - Lonely...

Thoughts about you weigh heavy on my mind
Thoughts of our love loss cuts me deep every time
I have many thoughts but the same conclusion
Without you all hope is gone...I'm losing
Now my heart beats but it feels so hollow
I LOST YOU...Such a hard pill to swallow
I miss your love and how it used to be
Now all alone I think of only Thee
So now when I dream it's of you only
Hoping you don't feel like I do...Lonely...

"HOT DOSE"

I did a Hot Dose, I feel the heat in my veins

Mom's should've killed me at birth by blowing out my damn brains

Last thing I remember was my life flashing by

And being scared as heck knowing that I'm about to die

High as heck off that Dose, I started seeing these visions

Of demons taunting me throughout my years spent in prisons

Telling me to screw "Life" and come reign in Hell

Because in Heaven they don't want Ex-Cons from jail

Come to Hell where it's fun, we're all schizophrenic

Because if there's blood to be spilled you know we're gonna spill it

Yo I feel it, I bite my tongue to try to stay awake

Because this is crazy!! I think I might have made a big mistake

At Heaven's Gate I know they'll never let me enter

Because besides the Devil I think I'm the worst of all sinners

And if there's rules to bend than I'm the rule bender

And my heart's gone cold...Colder than an Arctic Winter

But I remember someone once said to repent

And it will save your soul and make the Devil relent

Now my heart's beatin', and for the first time in my life

I hear GOD speakin', saying "COME TO THE LIGHT!!!"

He said, "Come with Me and all will be forgiven,

Choose Heaven now, because Hell is far worse than prison.."

Then I woke up, scared, like I seen a ghost

Now everyday's a fight to avoid that Hot Dose...I DID A HOT DOSE...

I did a Hot Dose, because I'm sick and deranged

All my life I've been high off speed, weed & cocaine

Last thing I remember was staring up at the sky

And feeling high as heck, just like I could fly

Right before my eyes I seen Heaven & Hell

Where they sent the Good and the ones who Rebel

But I was under the spell of this heroin dose

Being pulled up by Angels, and being pulled down by ghost

Then I made up my mind and tried to pull with the Angels

But then a demon grabbed my throat and I began to be strangled

I tried to shake him off, but he held on real hard

He dug his claws in my throat leaving a permanent scar

Feeling chills in my bones I start to shake and perspire

I seen The Tree Of Life , then seen The Lake Of Fire

Then I realized that I don't want to die

I know I don't deserve Heaven, but I don't want to fry

So I screamed out, "FATHER PLEASE SAVE MY SOUL!!!,

I DON'T WANNA DIE, FATHER PLEASE TAKE CONTROL!!!"

Then the Devil got mad, I felt the heat of the flames

Then I woke up at "Patton" strapped to a bed with chains

They said I tried to O.D. as all the doctors spoke

But they couldn't explain how I got that scar on my throat

Now every since that day I see Demons & Ghost

Choose Heaven or Hell, but don't choose that Hot Dose!!! I DID A HOT DOSE!!!

"ALONE"

Alone
Where has all the love gone
I'm so far away from home
The mirror has me scared to look upon
My face
Distorted and out of place
A blackjack hand of 20 but the dealer has a king and an ace
I can't keep up, I'm losing the race
So I come in last
A place where all your hopes are dashed
A place where no one remembers your a**
So now I can't move forward, but I can't escape the past
Now I find myself...Alone...

Alone
I've worked my fingers to the bone
My heart's a glass house at which people through stones
My love is strong but I have no one to call my own

For oh so long I've searched
And on my lonely nest I've perched
And I've even tried to flirt
But nothing seems to work
I feel so lost and it's a shame
I've come this far but now I wish I never came
I'm stuck in the fog, I'm stuck in the rain
Because I have been forsaken and left alone to face this pain
Alone...

I sit alone in a 4 cornered room staring at candles
Because my life is in turmoil and left in shambles
Locked up among killers, hoodlums, and violent vandals
I've gone crazy because this is a place a sane person just can't
handle
So take a look at my life and see what I see
MASS TRAGEDY - CATASTROPHE
Illegitimacy is now a way of life for me
With a P.H.D. in failure and a Doctorate in felonies
But through it all my heart still hasn't turned cold
Love is something that can't be bought or sold
Every soul is waiting for it's future to unfold
But no one want to be alone...If the truth be told Alone...

Alone
Life is colder than an ice cream cone
I need a team to get into the End Zone
But I'm on my own with both of my knees blown
It's hard to find the words when you don't know what to say
Longing to find true love is the greatest prayer I pray
The pain of being alone cuts me deeper everyday
And I'll sacrifice more than Jesus Christ if it will make
you stay
Look deep into my eyes to see the essence of "G-BONE"

But love is hard to come by since you've been gone
My life is like the saddest country song
What will you do when you've loss everything and find your-
self alone???
Alone...

"I STILL BELIEVE"

Every time I see your smile

It touches me deep within my spirit -

And I've been crying out for your love

But you never seem to hear it -

And the pain of it all

Is killing me...It's killing me -

But it your love

I still believe...I still believe -

And no matter where I find myself

No matter the time...No matter the place -

I'll do whatever it takes to be by your side

Because my greatest joy lives within the smile on your face -

But for reasons I can't understand I was blind-sided

This situation I could never foresee -

You took your smile away

And totally disappeared on me -

Now my joy is gone…I'm all alone

And my days are filled with sorrow & pain -

The pain of it all is unbelievable…UNBEARABLE

And this agony is far more than my poor soul can contain -

AND THE PAIN OF IT ALL

IS KILLING ME…IT'S KILLING ME -

BUT IN YOUR LOVE

I STILL BELIEVE…I STILL BELIEVE!!!

"BEFORE YOU"

Before You...
I saw my life
as lonely & hopeless -
But once you came into my life
you rearranged my focus -
To love & positivity
and because of you I know this -
So when I told you I love you
just know that it was real when I spoke it...

Before You...
My life was utter darkness
with no light in sight -
Pain & sorrow filled my days
loneliness & anguish gripped me at night -
But your presence within my life
has turned my darkness into light -
And given me the will to fight
for your love that made everything right...

Before You...
True Love in my life was always incomplete
past relationships left my heart bruised, black & blue -
And though "True Love" seemed out of reach
I would still continue to pursue -
But you came along and filled the breach which only your
love could do -
The depths of "LOVE" you continue to teach
but I never knew LOVE like this...BEFORE YOU...

"DON'T DO IT!!!"

I know life gets rough but you're no dummy
So don't get lost in the ruthless pursuit of money
Some sell drugs, others steal or rob
I just wish they'd put the same effort into trying to get a job
Many are impatient and greedy for gain
And in their illicit pursuit of money upon many they inflict
pain
You reason with yourself, "I'm only stealing to survive."
But every time you pull your weapon you could end up
taking many lives
The gun could accidentally discharge or that old lady could
have a heart attack
Many men are doing life in prison because they didn't
account for these facts
It seems like you're at the end of your rope and as far as
money you'll take your chances
Money is to be earned the right way and if you steal it there
will be dire consequences

Because once you get life in prison it's too late...YOU BLEW IT!!!
Please take heed to these words...DON' T DO IT!!!

What feels good now could really hurt you in the end
You're looking for love but passion left unchecked will lead to sin
And sin has a way of making sure that Death finds you
But you didn't think Death could come from someone that looks as good as she do
In the fierce persuasion of Lust's clutches you've got to have her this second
But they say it doesn't feel as good if you use that protection
Your temperature' s rising and you're caught up in the moment
You're not thinking with the right head because it feels so right, don't It
You want this girl to like you but you don't really know her
You just met her at the club tonight but you can' t see past your boner
And it seems like you' re at the end of your rope and as far as sex you'll take your chances
Sex can be a beautiful thing but if you don't use protection there can be dire consequences
Because once you catch "A.I.D.S." it's too late...YOU BLEW IT!!!
Please take head to these words...DON' T DO IT!!!

For every action there's a reaction
Either you're unfulfilled or there's satisfaction
If you squeeze that trigger what will happen
Will you survive the blast or be permanently nappin'
I'm telling you now that you shouldn't do it
You can be anything if you'd only pursue it

You can change the world with your talent if you'd only use it
And you mean the world to so many people but you never knew it
And I know it's easy to blame the world for your painful circumstances
Or blame the unchastity of your cheating Ex's that ruined all of your romances
And it may seem like you're at the end of your rope and as far as death you'll take your chances
Life is a gift and if you take it away there will be dire consequences
Because once yo u take your own life it's too late...YOU BLEW IT!!! Please take heed to these words...DON'T DO IT!!!

Epilogue:
Everything in life cost in one way or another
In the end all we have is love, life and respect for each other
For every great thing in life comes greater responsibility
And a chance to become greater than you ever thought you could be
Always remember that no one is below or above you
And never forget that GOD will always love you
You can be anything you want to be and GOD knew it
So when doubt tells you to give up...DON'T DO IT!!!

"I THINK IT'S TIME FOR A CHANGE"

Oh say can you see
Ain' t no freedom in this country for me
Innocent until proven guilty yet I've been locked up for over
10 years
Treated like an animal, I've cried so much I just tattooed my
tears
No cruel or unusual punishment is what the "Law" says
to me
Yet they will kill you on death row or permanently take you
away from your family
Freedom this - freedom that - is what this country speaks
Even freedom to do abominations to GOD...THIS SYSTEM
STINKS!!!
Convicted felons are no longer full Americans
Can't vote, bear arms, or fight for other Americans
And it's no wonder why people are angry in this so called
nation
Because there' s no rehabilitation, just permanent incar-
ceration

And you wonder why half the world has turned Gay or
Bisexual
These so called intellectuals don't even believe in GOD - I
find it odd
That we have more criminals and individuals that refuse
correction
A.I. D. S. is out there yet we still refuse to use protection
Everyone has an excuse
But no one ever gets to the root
Presidents promise everything but delivers nothing
LET ME SHOW YOU SOMETHING!!!
This country has trillions of dollars yet we have the world's
biggest debt
Where' s the love & hope, because in this country I've found
none yet
They made the Three Strikes Law, but oh now they regret
Because they didn't think they'd get life for that petty theft
I'll bet
What happened to the country indivisible under GOD
Our children are out of control because kids don't respect
parents who spare the "ROD"
I Think It's Time For A Change...

We've traded in our Slave Chains for hand cuffs
I know that minorities are strong enough, but they say we're
all uneducated cream puffs
At least when we were slaves we didn't kill each other
Because we knew all we had was GOD and one another
The Devil has found a new way to defeat the "Back Sliding
Man"
Give us life in prison with no shot at rehabilitation
Innocent men die on death row and it's a damn shame

After 400 years of slavery... Chains Still Remain!!!
I Think It's Time For A Change...

We've been hoodwinked, bamboozled, and led astray
For far too long in this country today
Why don't Teachers, Doctors or Parents have million dollar
contracts
These are the pillars of our communities and that's a fact jack
Don't just invest in our children, invest in all people as a
whole
Money makes the world go round but in the end we all
get old
Who will believe us when we say that we are changed men
Actions speak louder than words...Pride is a deadly sin
I Think It's Time For A Change...

My country tis' of thee
Land of Injustice & Misery To Thee I cringe!!!
Land where my people died
On drugs so their brains are fried
From every mountain side
The rich shall reign
I KNOW IT 'S TIME FOR A CHANGE!!!

"MS. SYPHILIS"

There ain't nothing sweet about my Ex-girl "Ms. Syphilis"
I thought it was all good until she stung me with her
bitter kiss
I still think of her sometimes when I reminisce
About the time she made blood and puss come out when I'd
piss...

When we had sex I liked the way you worked me
But in the end you really hurt me
Because I hit it "RAW-DOG" and you burnt me
And left my dick looking like beef jerky...

Yeah, that Syphilis girl is so cold
But she's got me hot with a fever and my head feels like it's
about to explode
You need to be locked up where guards patrolled
Because you've left me torn up and it hurts when I use the
commode...

DAMN!!! You've damn near broke me down to rigor mortis
Now I've got your infection coming out of every orifices
And I feel like a walking zombie from your diseased meta-
morphosis
But when I was sexin' you I didn't think I could croak from
this...

Young and wild I thought my demise would come from cap-
pillin'
But now "Ms. Syphilis" got me sick and it can't be cured with
sexual healin'
I guess you live and learn but only the infected know how I'm
feelin'
All I can say is thank GOD for Penicillin...

So I'm telling you brother use those condoms and don't hiss
Be careful who you lay with - Be careful who you kiss
And if you don't it might burn when you piss
Because you might be hooking up with my Ex-girl..."Ms.
Syphilis"...

"ESCAPE - (SOUL SEARCHING)"

All I do is give
All you do is take -
You're sucking up my soul
And making my heart break-
This is the result of letting sin in
And DEATH is the sinner's ultimate fate-
But I did this to myself
Yet it's myself that I can't ESCAPE...

With no where to go
And no one to turn to-
I've been running my whole life
Yet I could never escape you-
Sometimes it's you that I love
Sometimes it's you that I hate -
Without you I wonder how life would be
But without you nonexistence would be my fate -
Day by day, hour by hour
Minute by minute, second by second-

I try to learn from my mistakes
And count all my blessings -
I long to be like The Heavenly Father
With utter goodness and gracious through selflessness -
But I'm stuck within my sinful self
In a perpetual state of selfishness -
There's an inner turmoil growing deep within my soul
It makes me scared to look in the mirror-
I know I will see the reflections of a broken man
And the dread of The Specter of Death getting nearer...

All I do is give
All you do is take -
You're sucking up my soul
And making my heart break-
This is the result of letting sin in
And DEATH is the sinner's ultimate fate -
But I did this to myself
Yet it's myself that I can't ESCAPE...

"WELCOME TO THE WORLD OF TEARS"

Another bullied teenager shoots up a High School
Welcome to the world of madness -
Mothers grieve over their dead children
Welcome to the world of Sadness...
A wife calls the cops on her husband after he beat her
Welcome to the world of Domestic Violence -
A molested child won't tell because she' s scared
Welcome to the world of Suffering In Silence...
A cult leader has his followers thinking he's GOD
Welcome to the world of The Misguided -
A 12 year old girl is pregnant and her parents don't know
what to do
Welcome to the world of The Undecided...
A mother suffering from Postpartum Depression kills her
infant child
Welcome to the world of Tragedy -
A hooker O.D.'s on heroin and dies
Welcome to the world of Catastrophe...
A man robs a liquor store for money to keep getting high

Welcome to the world of Dope -
An innocent man on Death Row just lost his final appeal
Welcome to the world of No Hope...
Another teenager drops out of school unable to read or write
Welcome to the world of Illiteracy -
A man teaches his kids to hate people outside his race
Welcome to the world of Bigotry...
Many parents work 2 or 3 jobs but their kids won't even thank them for their sacrifice
Welcome to the world of The Unappreciated -
Many give their all to their mate only to be cheated on
Welcome to the world of Love Unreciprocated...
Thugs knock random people unconscious while playing The Knockout Game
Welcome to the world of A Wicked Deed -
A woman kills her husband for the life insurance money
Welcome to the world of Greed...
A mother snaps at her children for taking too long to come when she called
Welcome to the world of Impatience -
Through Adam's sin Satan has unleashed Hell on Earth
Welcome to the world of Damnation...
With Satan at the controls we have his demons to lead the nations
Welcome to the world of your Worst Fears -
And with his minions to unleash Havoc on the Earth
WELCOME TO THE WORLD OF TEARS!!!

Epilogue:
In the state of this world how con anyone make it Things are getting worse, how can anyone take it
For each person there's a different world - A different dimension
The sad thing is we destroy ourselves and make our worlds

hard to live in We must change our ways to give a brighter future to our boys 8 girls

So it can truly be a greeting when we say, "Welcome to our world..."

"INSINCERE"

I didn't want to believe the absolute fact
That you would turn on me and not have my back
When I was on top by my side you sat
But then you got ghost as soon as I fell flat...

You were my constant companion throughout the years
You were the one that I trusted to wipe away my tears
You were the only one I'd die for out of all my peers
Now in my troubles I cry to you for help, but it fell on deaf
ears...

Who would have believed my best friend would turn
And leave me in the flames of tribulations to burn
Because your thinking process I really can't discern
Now I trust no one...That's the lesson I've learned...

Now I'm thinking of what I can do to make it better
So I write you, but get no reply to my letters

And to think I thought we had a bond that nothing could sever
But now my heart has been torn in two forever...

And it's so cold out here alone, I want you back by my side
But I feel so betrayed...This is a pain I just can't hide
If I said I don't miss you anyone who looked at me would know that I lied
Forget my pride - I shed tears, but you don't even care that I cried...

For me I thought you cared...I really wanted to believe it
I gave you my hand in friendship...But you never truly received it
You turned your back on me...This day I never thought I would see it
Because you said you loved me...But now you've shown that you don't mean it...

Now I pray for redemption but does GOD hear???
Because being on my own has always been my greatest fear
Without you I've cried a sea and I'm drowning in my tears
Never to recover from knowing that your love was INSINCERE...

"BON APPETIT"

It's so convenient - The Drive-Thru
But you didn't realize that it's killing you
If the truth be told it's really a "DIE-THRU"
Making you morbidly obese... Now who you gonna cry to???

Right before your eyes - Your body's gaining size
This fact can't be denied - But by the time you realize
That It's poison that they hide - Inside those burger & fries
And millions "Super-Size" - Their way to an early demise...

Our foods are now filled with hormones & pesticides but
most don't see
That in the name of mass production these foods are killing
you & me
It affects our kids in that at age 7 or 8 they're already showing
sighs of puberty
With Diabetes, high blood pressure & cardiovascular disease
resulting from mass obesity...

So much of our food is processed, now ain' t that something
And don't let me get started on microwave food...A little radiation never hurt nothing
It's hard to find natural foods and most of our delicacies are so disgustin'
They have the nerve to call it " Gourmet" as they poison you at your luncheon...

With overindulgence, over -access & over-eating you' re gaining weight every night
And with having kids, poor diet & lack of exercise, doesn't your belt feel tight???
With M.S.G., food coloring & processed foods we're being poisoned left & right
And with lack of physical activity our metabolism slows down with every bite...

We're so bombarded with unhealthy choices of food constantly in our face
We can't even remember how healthy food is supposed to taste
This has been going on so long there's only so much that o ur bodies can take
Until our bodies shut down and an early grave is our fate...

So keep on keeping on eating fried foods and pig feet
Blinded by fast food because healthy food most people won't seek
I bet you never thought what you put into your stomach would mean your demise & defeat
So think about that before the next time you eat..."Bon Appetit..."

"MAN'S FALLEN STATE"

Whenever it rains I believe the sky is crying
Could it be because of Man's destructive nature or because
the world is dying

Who would have ever thought that when GOD created Man
That we would turn out so terrible - That we would destroy
GOD's plans

People kill people - It's not the fault of the gun
Governments build weapons of mass destruction leaving no
place to run

Every since Cain & Able we've found reasons to hurt each
other
Why do we believe The Devil's lies - Why can' t we see that
we' re all sisters & brothers

It goes back to The Garden of Eden and Adam & Eve

Where Adam relented to sin and Eve blamed it on being deceived

How could they do this after tasting GOD's utter goodness
He gave them the absolute best and yet they still forsook it

Now all of creation is living in a fallen state
Where Satan rules the world - Where the law of the land
is HATE

People don't want reconciliation they just want revenge
But if GOD dealt with us the same way all life would end

At some point we all need mercy
But it's man's refusal to love and obey GOD that always
hurts me

So I ask all people to accept GOD' s ways and His wise
knowledge
And rebuke The Devil with all his lies that are full of garbage

Haven't you ever wondered why GOD saved the lives of you
and me? ??
It's because He loves us...We're His kids...We're His Family!!!

Love and forgiveness is GOD's gift to Man...If we'd only
receive it
Nothing's impossible with GOD...If you'd only believe it

Now we've come full circle back to Adam and Eve' s fatal
mistake
Only GOD can do the impossible...Which is repair Man from
his fallen state...

"WHEN TIME STANDS STILL"

I was living in darkness in search of light

Until the day you walked into my life

Where once there was sadness your smile instantly changed how I was feeling

And everywhere I was broke your love brought supernatural healing

From the first time our eyes met

It seems like the sands of time halted and the clock ceased to tick

Purified love is what I felt in the enormity of that moment

It's what I always longed for and every since all I've ever wanted

Now every time I look at you it's like I've ascended to the heavens

Where time has no place - There's no hours, minutes or seconds

In you Heaven is all I see - It's as if your presence is the key

To the place of eternity - Which is the only place I want to be

I don't know what it is but every time our eyes interlock

I get lost in your aura and the procession of time seems to stop

And in that moment you outdo, outshine and exceed all that I want or need

And turned all my hopes and dreams into something I can truly believe

In you I've found the greatest of all treasures...The "Agape Love" of GOD

I never thought I'd get rid of all my resentments, but your spirit did the job

Every time I look at you mere words can't express the joy I feel

Because every time I look at you...THAT'S WHEN TIME STANDS STILL...

"ALTERNATE REALITY"

You take me to an alternate reality
To a place where there's just you and me
To a place beyond the physical
To a love that's deep and spiritual
You've touched my soul
And made me lose all control
Because on this plain of blissful existence
To your love I offer no resistance
I now live in your love and it's light
There's no more pain or reason to fight
I'm now beyond space & Time, beyond latitude & longitude
I've been transcended with pure LOVE or the highest
magnitude
Now you're my dreams at night
You're my sunlight
You make all my wrongs right
And you've taken all darkness out of my life
Now your love is all I see
From within the sphere of this Alternate Reality...

"MY INCURABLE SORROW"

Every since the day I was born - I've been going through the
storm
For me sorrow is the norm - I live in a world more perverted
than porn...

If you could feel my pain than you'll know what I'm going
through
But there's no greater pain than losing the love of you...

You left me burnt - Baptized me in the flames
Yet I find it strange - That you don't feel my pains...

When I look in the mirror what do I see
The reflections of a man in total agony...

I have so many questions and I'm left wondering why
If there's a GOD up above why does He let love die???

Because I've been going through so many changes and it's left
me leery
I guess there's no mercy for the weak and no rest for the
weary...

My life is so bleak that I look towards my own demise with
gladness
How can I go on when all hope is gone and my heart is filled
with sadness???

Pure madness, I'm on the verge of insanity
Because I'm going through HELL and there's no one here to
save me...

I've tried to be strong, but the tears keep raining down
And I've cried out for relief, but no one seems to hear the
sound...

Now I've loss control of my every emotion
And I can't find peace in this world full of commotion...

How much more of this suffering must I endure
Because suffering brings Death when left to fester and
mature...

My afflictions today makes me scared to face tomorrow
And I wouldn't wish upon anyone to face My Incurable
Sorrow...

"DEATH'S DOOR"

When you're looking at Death's Door
You're scared to go through not knowing what's in store
Now you notice things that you never noticed before
Like the sheer terror of Death that now you can't ignore
Just thinking about being 6 feet under the floor
Shakes your mind, body & soul to the core
Now that you're faced with knowing "Death" is not a myth, fable or lore
And once that reality sets in it horrifies you even more
You want to live so for your life you beg, plead & implore
Devastated, you say,"I'll go through now...What are you waiting for???"
Then Death's Door opens, your life flashes by and you see
Life & Death at war
This is what happens at the end of life when you're looking at "Death's Door"

"THERE WAS YOU"

When I thought I couldn't take it
When I thought I wouldn't make it
When I ran out of patience
There Was You...

When my heart was steady breakin'
And my love was turning to hatin'
When I thought I'd been forsaken There Was You...

When the world left me weary And Life left me dreary
Because when I pray it seems no one hears me There Was
You...

When sorrow had been my daily liaison And I've been in
pain for so long
When it seemed all hope was gone There Was You...

When betrayal left me irate

Then long sleepless nights made me hallucinate And when suicidal thoughts threaten to overtake There Was You...

When I need help you can always tell
Your spirit alone can help mine soar and sail I LOVE YOU!!!
Because when all else failed THERE WAS YOU...

"BECAUSE OF YOU"

From the love inside of you
You take me to heights I never knew
When the chips are down you always come through
Because you're a friend tried & true...

There's a light within your spirit that leaves me beaming It's
always your smile that I see whenever I'm dreaming
When all seemed hopeless you kept me believing
And it's the love that we share which gives my life meaning...

Looking into your heart I can see Love, Joy & Honesty
As well as Strength, Diligence & Generosity
And on my best day I could never match your inner beauty...

You're so talented, intelligent & real
You've shown me how to embrace life with true zeal
Mere words can't express how special you make me feel
That's why I love you and always will...

I love you and all that you do
Deeper than friends or family is us two
You've shown me the intricacies of love that I never knew
Now I'm in Perpetual Euphoric Bliss...Because Of You...

"TORN"

I stand before you torn...
Torn between glad and sad
Torn between good and bad
Torn between mom and dad
Torn between want and had
Torn between oddness and normalcy
Torn between who I am and who I need to be TORN...

I stand before you torn...
Torn between the day and the night
Torn between the dark and the light
Torn between what's wrong and what's right
Torn between happiness and fright
Torn between oddness and normalcy
Torn between who I am and who I ought to be TORN...

I stand before you torn...
Torn between regretful and great
Torn between demonic and saint

Torn between could and cain't
Torn between what is and what ain't
Torn between oddness and normalcy
Torn between who I am and who I long to be TORN...

I stand before you torn...
Torn between real and fake
Torn between fact and fate
Torn between love and hate
Torn between Heaven and Hell's Gate
Torn between oddness and normalcy
Torn between who I am and who I always wanted to be
TORN...

Epilogue:
So tear me up until I'm torn and shredded like confetti
We all want to live forever but LORD knows we're not ready
Look at yourself and you'll see like me you're torn
It's hard to love everyone when in return you're lovelorn
Because in each person there's an inner war they must fight
Torn between the darkest of evils and the pure righteousness
of light
TORN...

"THE PROMISE"

When bullets fly - People die
Mothers cry - And everyone's left wondering why

Your whole life flashes before your eyes in a split second
Then you' re left wondering why GOD left you without His
protection

With the flick of a finger everything rearranges
And when bullets hit you it's funny how your priorities
changes

Things like food, friends and rent no longer matter
Because at that moment how to survive is the only thing
you're after

The bullets in your flesh burns like fire
The pain is intense and now you feel cold, yet you still
perspire

You start to hallucinate about your life and everything you did Your whole life in reverse from adult-teenager-to a little kid

Then you see the "Angel Of Death" approaching, but to you he' s a demon
Then he says to you,"Why should I let you live? Give me a good reason..."

So you say,"I've worked hard, I pay taxes, I've been good in life!!"
But he says,"You've been greedy, You've lied, stole and cheated on your wife."

I know all your dirty secrets and there's nothing that I didn't see,
And the good didn't outweigh the bad so now you must come with me!!!"

So he touches your forehead and everything goes black with no sound
Now you' re standing before GOD in dread knowing that it's about to go down

All of your sins come to mind and It's left your spirit crushed and mangled
GOD says,"Depart from Me, you cursed into everlasting fire prepared for the Devil and his angels!"

Then you scream as your skin blisters in the torment of the flames
You plead, "Heavenly Father if you gave me another chance I PROMISE I would change!!"

Then in the blink of an *eye* you awake perfectly fine but drenched in sweat
And you hear GOD's voice saying,"Remember your PROMISE...Don't ever forget!!!"

HAIKU:

"Winter/Spring/Summer/Fall"

Haiku: "Winter"
With grey snow filled clouds Winter so bitterly cold Snow
falling...White Gold

* * *

Haiku: "Spring" Sunshine - The wind blows
Smell the flowers - It's spring time The Butterfly knows

* * *

Haiku: "Summer"
It's hot as fish grease
As solar flares hit the air Summertime is here

* * *

Haiku: "Fall" Dawn of a new day
Leaves are now falling I see Fall amazes me

"THE LUSTFUL CHEATER"

You've got me feeling so low
How could you do me so cold

Even after all you put me through
I was still there for you

Now I'll never be the same
How could love hurt and have me in so much pain

Well I guess it wasn't love at all
Yet I'm still on my knees - Watch me crawl

No matter how I begged - No matter how I pleaded
You left me suffering with no way to ease it

Life is so hard but relationships are even harder
And now I wonder why we even bothered

How could you be so beautiful and yet make me cry

It was your bad attitude that made my pains multiply

Because love is patient - Love is kind
But you couldn't leave your selfishness and pride behind

Now I'm in a state of shock - Almost comatose
But it's the fact that you lied & cheated that hurts me the most

Young and naive, I was easy to manipulate
Now I see that dealing with your "B.S." for so long was a BIG
mistake

Because you shattered all my dreams being a phony who
couldn't stay true
You've mixed my indignation double with your betrayal
times two

Like the Devil you feed off sin - You're a "SIN EATER"
The path way blazed to HELL is lead by you - The Lustful
Cheater...

"THE NEXT LEVEL"

I wanna take our relationship to the next level
Kiss you on your naked navel
Hold you and never let go
Because in your arms is where Love flows...

I wanna fulfill your wildest dreams
Do so many sensual things
Watch me as I paint this scene
To make your toes curl as I make you scream...

When you put your lips on mine I lose all track of time
You always blow my mind
When we're together ecstasy ain't hard to find...

Well you know my style which is cool, calm and mellow
And usually I like to stay on the straight and narrow
I wanna try some new things so please don't think I'm an odd
fellow

Because Baby I wanna get freaky and take us to the next level...

"THE APOLOGY"

I was a fool to do you so wrong
But I'll be a fool for you if you'll come back home

I'm so sorry because I know I let you down
And when you needed me most I was never around

Papa I'm sorry - I know you taught me to be a better man
Life doesn't always turn out how you plan - I hope one day
you'll understand

Mama I'm sorry - Sorry for all the wrong I've done
I know I should have been a better son - If there's anyone I
love you're the 1

Brother I'm sorry - I should have shown you a better way
And told you that I love you everyday - But my pride got in
the way

Sister I'm sorry - I know for you I've never been there

I know that wasn't fair - But I want you to know that I care

To My Family - I've never known a greater bunch
Each one of you has left me touched - Your love to me means
so much

I'm so sorry because I know my actions harmed Thee
I hope that you all will forgive me and accept this Apology...

"LOVE NURTURED"

I've been knowing you for so long

How could things go so wrong

Now I'm singing sad songs

Because now you're gone

And you've left my mind blown

I've never felt a Love so strong

I loved your voice's sweet tone

It'd send chills down my bones...

Because you're my Angel

I can see you shining with your halo

You always seem to turn the tables

And now I'm willing and able

To hold you and never let go

Because in your presence Love seems to flow

That's why I love you and I'm here to let you know

That I'm here to nurture your love to make sure that it grows...

"WAITING FOR GOD TO COME"

In the end there's no escape because from your fate you can't run
Because we're all waiting for GOD...Waiting For GOD To Come...

No one ever seems to get it right
Because we're all struggling to make it through this thing called "Life"
To get to the top you have to scratch and fight
And we've all searched for GOD but he's hidden from our sight...

What can you do when you've given your all
And once you've hit rock bottom how much further can you fall
When I think about the future I wanna pause - I wanna stall
And I hope I don't hear it...Whenever Death calls...

All of my life I've been a witness to destruction, terror &
mayhem
There's a thin line between Love & Hate, being Blessed and
being Damned
Who do you believe in...GOD or in man???
I wonder if religion is real or just a big shame...

I've asked many people why they still believe
In a GOD they haven't met or even perceived
I have so many questions with some doubts I can't defeat
I find it odd that I searched my whole life and yet found
nothing concrete...

I've had dreams of Heaven and glorious days
But I wake up to pain and the sorrow stays
Does GOD really hear when a sinner prays
Is there really hope for a sinner if he changes his ways???

It baffles my mind so I rack my brain
GOD if you hear me...WHY DID YOU CREATE PAIN???
I love sunshine and I endure the rain
How can GOD love us if we don't think the same???

In the end there's no escape because from your fate you
can't run
Because we're all waiting for GOD...WAITING FOR GOD TO
COME...

"AN ANGEL'S TOUCH"

I can see rainbows when I look into your eyes
And every time I see your heart I'm amazed by it's size

Time has a way of changing us, but for me one thing stays
the same
It's the fact that I love you, and that will never change

I'll always love you and all that you do
I'll fight any demon - Go through Hell Fire for you

Did you know when we're alone, for me, time stands still
And at that moment I know I'm alive and that Love is real

There's no substitute for you - Nothing else will over do
The sad thing is you never knew - That you were my dream
come true

Your smile sets my heart on fire and fills me with desire
Then my breath quickens and I start to perspire

Your skin tone sends chills down my bones
I fantasize about your ecstatic moans when I kiss your erotic zones

Utter bliss ends in bitterness
Whenever I reminisce about the end of our first kiss

Because there's no greater feeling than sexual healing
And I'll take you there...If you're willing

It's easy to get lost in the joy of your laughter
You're like Heaven in human form, but now I wonder what comes after

I just wish the world knew you or the love I've become used to
For if they did they'd all pursue you and never do anything to lose you

In the end it's your Love, Humility and inner beauty that means so much
If only everyone could feel the love of YOU...An Angel's Touch...

"CHOICES"

Life is all about choices

They're made in your head, can't you hear the voices

You can choose to live or die

You can give up or choose to try

You can be a thug and choose to hold a grudge

Or you can choose to forgive and show love

You can choose to do wrong or do right

You can choose to remain in darkness or come into the light

You can choose to work hard to gain success

Or you can choose to be lazy and continue to digress

You can choose to learn from the wise where Wisdom is received

Or you can choose to fall into foolishness by not taking heed

You can choose to live and let live

You can choose to receive or to give

You can choose to be loyal or betray

You can choose to stay or go away

You can choose to be real or to be fake

You can choose to destroy or create

With so many choices how can we ever decide

We all choose how we live but not how we died

It's all done in our heads, can't you hear the voices

No fate is certain...It all depends on your choices...

"MY ANGEL DIVINE"

Many may search but never find

A love like yours...My Angel Divine... I wanna go on walks
with you

I wanna sit and talk with you I wanna do what Lovers do

But it seems that you never knew

And no matter what tomorrow brings

As long as you're by my side I'll be smiling

You give me pleasures I've never known

You give me the strength to carry on

And when others didn't give a damn

You never left me forsaken

And when I was crumbling under Life's demands

You showed me mercy and that you understand

When my life turned down an ugly highway

You appeared to beautify me

And even when I did you so wrong

You never left me alone

You forgave me every time

Because your nature is so kind

And many may search but never find

A love like yours...My Angel Divine...

"SOMETIMES"

Sometimes I can't sleep at night
Wondering why I can't get it right
Wondering what's the purpose of my life
I mean what more must I sacrifice???

Sometimes I close my eyes knowing things aren't always
what they seem
Hoping my life's nightmare is just another bad dream
Hoping I don't fall for any of the Devil's schemes
So I avoid the hoodlums, criminals and dope fiends...

Sometimes I wonder what truly lives in the heart of men
Are we all doomed to fail because of Adam's sin
Are we all phonies and fakes who front and pretend
Sometimes I wonder will pain and sorrow ever end???

Sometimes I wonder why GOD is so hard to find
And why is Love and Hate divided by such a thin line

So I read the Good Word and look for Revelation's warning signs
In the end it'll either be your soul or mine...

Sometimes I wonder what happens at Life & Death crossroad
And between Heaven & Hell which way do you go
I mean what's the source of Hatred and why does it flow
Only time will tell if we will ever know

Sometimes I get lonely And I think of you only
But now you act like you don't know me Was our friendship full of baloney???

Sometimes I feel so lost that I'm engulfed in darkness where no light shines
And it seems around every corner there's monsters of various kinds
Like the ones who crucified "Jesus" and convicted Him of false crimes
And it proves even the best of us have to suffer...Sometimes...

"YOUR LOVE"

Without you there is no me

We're two peas in a pod, our love was meant to be

And when my world filled with danger and pain is all I see

Your Love holds the key to come and rescue me...

When all else fails I can call on you

You've got my back and always make sure I make it through

Our heart's beat as one even though they're two

You are my heart's greatest desire but it seems you never knew...

Your Love is priceless, more precious than gold

Your Love is priceless, it can't be bought or sold

Your Love is priceless, it never gets old

I need Your Love, to have and to hold...

Your Love is all I need to get by

Your Love is all I need to get high

Your Love makes me believe I can fly

Because my love for you just won't die...

I love Your Love so please don't change

Because Your Love took away all of my pain

I hope my love for you does the same

Your Love gives me peace in a world that's gone insane...

Together we fit like a glove

So lets fly away on the wings of a dove

Because you're my Angel that was sent from above

Pure Joy - Pure Heaven - Pure Perfection...That's Your Love...

"BLACK INVENTORS"

Black Inventors have so greatly improved this nation

Where would we be without all of their creations

Like George Crum who invented potato chips

But I bet you never thought about him when you put one to your lips

Or like Lonnie Johnson who invented the Super Soaker

Yeah he was black, but I bet no one ever told ya

I bet you never thought about Thomas Tennings to get your clothes fresh

He' s the one who invented the Dry Cleaning Process

Every Winter you should give thanks to David Crosthwait

Because he invented Heating Installations that keep warmth in your place

Think of Joseph Hawkins every time you use your oven

He created Metal Oven Racks, now ain't that somethin '

Many heart patients can thank Otis Boykin for their heart's beat

Because he invented a Control Unit for the Pacemaker, now ain' t that neat

The military can thank Benjamin Bradley for creating a powerful Steam Engine

Because they used them on warships to go on war missions

Think of Daniel McCree and all the lives he saved He created the Fire Escape

Elijah McCoy invented an Automatic Lubricating Cup and for trains it was pure joy

He was held in such high regard that he coined the phrase "The Real McCoy"

And Garrett Morgan was one of the most prolific inventors of the past

With inventions such as a Hair Straightener, Automatic Traffic Signal & Gas Mask

Patricia Bath created a Laser to perform surgery for cataracts

But if you don' t look back in history you will never know these facts

Black Inventors have changed history with a personal touch

And have been personally responsible for why we have so much

So know your history and know your facts

Because the things we enjoy so much might have just been invented by someone black

And make sure you give thanks and always remember

To give props and respect to all of our Black Inventors...

"BABY MAMA"

I'm tired of all this drama
All you do is scream and holla
I swear I wish you weren't my Baby's Mama
Now child support is taking all of my dollars

A lion tamer couldn't even tame ya
I get no love, but you show more love to complete strangers
It's like you get a kick out of sending me through changes
Because you let your fierce wrath rearrange us

And even though we're no longer together you still put me
through the strain
Every time I see you I'm instantly in pain
I show you respect but you refuse to give me the same
How could I have ever been involved with such a dizzy dame

Baby Mama look at all the foul stuff you did Fussing and
fighting right in front of the kids
That's why when I seen you coming my way I hid

Because if I reacted to your "B.S." I'd end up doing a jail bid

It kills me inside to know that I got involved
With a crazy woman that even made me lose my job
Every night with you was a boxing match where I had to
weave and bob
You break me down to damn near rigor mortis and it's my
spirit that you robbed

When I finally got the guts to say it's over you keyed my car
Everyday was a battle with you that's left my heart so scared
But at least now I can see you for who you really are
I just wish things didn't have to go this far

So now I roll down the street in my keyed Chevy Impala
And I'm trapped because to see my kids I have to call her
So I'm stuck in the trauma and have to deal with the drama
Because a man's worst nightmare is none other than...His
Baby Mama...

"THE GAME OF LOVE"

In this game of love I hope I don't blow it
Because you set my heart on fire and I didn't even know it
And the pain is so deep that I can' t even control it
It's left my heart torn in two, now I' m trying to re -sow it...

The game of love is full of ups & downs, sometimes joy -
sometimes drama
And I'm looking for a wife not just a baby mama
But I always end up with a crazy woman that wants to cuss
and holla
And upon the ashes of another broken relationship I' m left
alone to deal with the trauma...

I never thought the game of love could be so cold
Everyone seems to cheat, and a selfish lover very quickly
gets old
But if I may be so bold - I'm looking for a woman with a heart
of gold

One from where love always flowed - To be my rock, to have and to hold...

The game of love is not for the faint of heart
It can utterly tear your soul apart
And it never seems like that from the start
So you should be careful and take it slow if you' re smart...

The game of love can end in joy or end in pain It can feel like sunshine or rain
Sometimes you'll have feelings that you can't explain
With Love you get what you give, so give love and hope in return you' ll get the same...

"WHEN THE LOVE IS GONE"

I wanted you to feel me - I wanted you to understand
I wanted you to see the real me - I wanted to be your man

And although we're apart - I long to be where you are
And although you broke my heart - I'll come to you no matter how far

Why do you cause me so much pain - But to provide for you I hustle
Why do I go through this strain - It' s like you love to tussle

It's like we're poison for each other - But you're my child's mother
But now I've discovered - That my anguish can't he covered

Because this ain't love - This is dread
Rather than push and shove - I'll just leave instead

But as I turn to go - You punched me in the head

And then gave me a look to let me know - That you wish I were dead

How did it come to this - How could you get so pissed
To spit in my face and hiss - With the same mouth I used to kiss

How could you make your beautiful face - Frown up and distort out of place
So I run away and you gave chase - Now I feel like less of a man in total disgrace

And to think I worked my fingers to the bone - To provide you with a home
How did things go so wrong - I'm a man that's scared to answer my own phone

I'm done with all this scrappin' - Because I'm better off alone
And this is what happens - When The Love Is Gone...

"UNLOVED"

I never wanted to hurt you
But you piss me off from the things that you do

I never thought it would come to this
Instead of a compliment and a kiss
You gave me a shove and a diss
And said on my grave you would piss
Then straight in my face you spit
But it was my heart that took the hit

You cursed me out in the worst way
Never thought we'd see this day

Because it's like a knife in my windpipe
I swear I can't breathe after we fight

And I try to say to myself that you didn't mean it
And every time you say you're sorry I wanted to believe it

But actions speak louder than words
Now my family and friends are telling me to kick you to the curb

But I'm too blind to see that all you do is tell lies
They say love is blind, but I can't see anything with these tears in my eyes

Together we're like an earthquake mixed with a hurricane - Total Disaster
LOVELORN - You treat me like a Ghetto Bastard

Now I'm stuck in a dilemma that I can't see through
Do I stay in this painful relationship or just leave you

It takes two to tango, but it also takes two to argue You've hurt me, but now I must leave before I harm you

You've loss me forever, so I fly away like a dove Never to return to this feeling of being "Unloved..."

"MY ANGEL-MY ALL-MY DESTINY"

No matter the time - No matter the place
I always long to see your smiling face

Because in my heart I know it's true
My love belongs to only you

For Valentine's Day - Throughout time - And always
Our love is deeper than cards, candy or flowers could
ever say

To hold you in my arms would mean so much
I'd get lost in the rapture of your touch

Because I love you and I hope the whole world knows
And over time my love for you continuously grows

You're beautiful inside and out - From your head to your toes
And I'm the happiest person in the world because I'm the one
you chose

I love your laughter and you captivate me with your smile
You're my one true love, I've known this for a while

Now all I see is your love and it's simply amazing
At first there was a spark but now our passion is blazing

For your love I'll pay the ultimate price because you're worth
saving
I'll give my life in exchange for yours and I ain't playing

Because your happiness means everything to me
Your beauty shines inside and out, and anyone who met you
would have to agree

That you're Love purified and you were sent here to be My
Angel - My All - My Destiny...

"WHEN I PAUSE FOR A MINUTE"

There's been times in my live when I pause for a minute
And thought about how my life would be without you in it...

Everyday of my life would be one big sad song Because there
would be no joy if you were gone...

Everyday would turn to night if you weren't within sight
And then I'd start drinking and end up in a bar fight...

With you I feel so tall, but with you gone I'd feel so small
Because you always have my back, but with you gone who
else can I call???

I'd definitely miss your smile, and your voice's soft tone
I could build a house, but without you it'd be no home...

At night I couldn't sleep - I would toss and turn
I'd be too scared to find someone else - Afraid of getting
burned...

In a moments time I'd look for a sign
Of how someone so kind could leave me behind...

There's so many things I'd miss - I have an endless list
Like thoughts of when we'd kiss - Whenever I'd reminisce...

Because you're so stunning - So provocative
You keep my heart drumming - You've shown me how to
Truly Live...

That's why when I think of your heart I'll do anything to
win it
And these are the things that I ponder...When I Pause For A
Minute...

"LEARNING TO SWIM"

While at the swimming pool I dive in on a whim
And then I begin to reminisce about how I first learned to
swim...

I remember my sisters would race and while I watched
I'd pretend That I was racing too and I would always win...

I started in 3 feet, that's where I began
But my pride wanted me to swim in the deep end...

I already had dreams of putting swimming trophies on the
mantel
But at this point the "doggy Paddle" was more than I could
handle...

Trying to be a "Big Boy" I tried to swim but just went down
then water got in my nose and I damn near drowned...

I was lucky that my sisters were there to save me every time

But I was determined to swim - I had made up my mind...

So I kept at it and finally learned to Doggy Paddle
And soon even swimming in the deep end was something I
could handle...

Then the next thing you know I learned to dive and do flips
No longer afraid I'd drown because I could swim like a fish...

And even though I didn't grow up to be an Olympic class
swimmer
I always have fond thoughts of learning to swim when I
remember...

"I'M TIRED OF THE BULLSH" T!!!"

Guys cheatin' - Girls cheatin'

People killin' - People stealin'

Drug deal in' - Cap pillin'

I've searched for love - But no one's willin'

We need better schools - But they just build better prisons

There's always charity - But less is given

For the rich love is bought and sold - But underneath the heart is cold

Our children are out of control - They don' t even respect the old

There's no loyalty, all bonds are severed - Will Hate burn forever???

I wonder why it takes a tragedy to unite - And bring us all together

Many are forced to rob - When all they wanted was a job

The system is a fraud - And we as a society will ostracize him...Ain' t That Odd??!!

If you're wrong you're wrong - But haven't we all at some point been wrong??

For many pain is their only song - Look at the world today, I think Love is gone Like Marvin Gaye

I wonder what's going on - You can work your fingers to the bone

But our streets aren't safe and neither our home - Only one can save us...GOD alone...

The heart is so cold and eclectic - Filled with so many things unexpected

It can turn you evil if you neglect it - But a good heart is always respected

From the beginning everything that man has touched ended up corrupted

Adam was in paradise but The Tree Of Good & Evil...He Just Had To Touch it!!!

So he believed the serpents lie, but ultimately it was the "Greed" inside

It all starts in the eye, t he eye is like fire ...It' s never satisfied

And that's why we all sin, and have never been able to quit

I wonder will it ever end, because I'm Tired Of The Bullsh*t!!!

"A MAN AIN'T SUPPOSE TO CRY"

I know a man ain't suppose to cry
But this pain that I feel can't be denied
I thought I was a better man with you by my side
And to this day I don't know why you lied

What more can I do or say
Because you've damaged me in a major way
Now my dreams are shattered and I'm cursed when I pray
And I'm scared to face tomorrow if it's going to be like today

You've left my heart on fire and filled with pains
And the tears I've cried can't put out the flames I was serious,
but you were playing games
Because my heart was crushed when we made love and you
called out other names

Now a cloud of sorrow surrounds me
Now a lonely heart is what I'll be
Now I'm trying to survive this dire tragedy

And the sad thing is you never TRULY cared about me

But I was too blind to see you stabbing me in the back
And I didn't know that Truth & Sensitivity was something
that you lacked
It's like you took my heart and chopped it up with an axe
I've been done wrong in the past but you've taken it to
the max

Now every time I think of you I whimper and I sigh
And I can't live like this, but I'm too afraid to die
You've left me looking for answers and wondering why
And I've shed countless tears even though they say a man
ain't suppose to cry

"BELIEVE IN ME"

Believe in me and I'll be there

Believe in me because I care

While others treated you like a doormat I would never
do that

Just trust that I'm here to save Ya

Believe in me and I'll be your savior

I know that the world left a scar on your heart

And Life's struggles seem to tear your joy apart

When all seems hopeless and the pain left your face with a
frown

Believe in me because I won't let you down

I Love You - That's A Fact

I Love You - Please Believe That

I used to believe that love doesn't cost a thing

But now I know that love can cost you everything

And for you I'm willing to make that sacrifice

Because True Love is what I have for you...The whole point of Life

So believe in me when times get tough

Believe in me when times get rough

Believe in me and that my love is good enough

Because knowing you believe in me means so much

I'm here to show you how Love's supposed to be

Just as long as you...Believe In Me...

"SHINE"

My friend You've been on my mind

I've been thinking about how bright you shine

You Shine like a diamond

So beautiful you left me cryin'

You shine brighter than the rising sun

You shine like the stars in The Heavens

You're one of a kind - A beauty like none other

You stay on my mind - The full depths of your beauty I have yet to discover

Every time I see you all I can say is "WOW!!!"

Your beauty hurts so good, "OUCH!!!"

It's the sparkle in your eyes - The brilliance of your skin

The glow of your teeth - And a smile that transcends

To live in the presence of your radiance would be enough

Because within the light of your presence is the culmination of Love

You're the Love & Light of my world and you illuminate my Soul & Mind

And when all else fails your Love won't...Because You Shine...

"LOVE IS ABSTRACT"

Love is sometimes selfish -
But most times love is selfless,
Love is the air I breath -
But at times Love left me breathless...

Love is why we were given life -
Love can be explosive like dynamite,
Love is the source of universal light -
Love is the whole point of Life...

Love is deeper than the oceans & seas -
Love can bring the strongest man to his knees, Love is the
cure for a broken heart's disease -
Love is the best of us for it is what GOD sees...

Sometimes love doesn't cost a thing - That's Free Love -
At other times it can cost you everything -
That's Sacrificial Love,
Love in it's infancy - That's Puppy Love -

Love's rod of correction - That's Tough Love...

Love...So much joy when you're in it -
Love...So much pain when it ended,
Love...For you, my last dime I would spend it -
Love...We all want to win it...

Love is much deeper than just a sex act -
Because Love is the very substance that holds all of creation
intact,
There's so many levels of Love...This is a fact -
Love is limitless...Love is Abstract...

"ALWAYS"

I've been crying myself to sleep, and my heart' s been torn
apart
Because without you I'm incomplete, and life seems so dark

Loneliness has overtaken me - Every since you've
forsaken me
Less of a man is what you' re making me - And without your
love Life is breaking me

I feel sorrow when I look out the window pane
Then I look at your picture but my feelings don' t change

When I dream of you it' s more of the same thang
I see your face everywhere and knowing we are apart fills my
heart with pain

I really thought we were meant to be
I wish the love I have for you was felt mutually

If you could look into my heart then you would see The
purity of the love that I have for Thee

I miss you more and more each day
With so many things unsaid that I wish I could say

I haven' t always been believer but on bended knee I pray
For you to return and to love me like I love you...Always...

"OUR LOVE WILL ALWAYS BE"

You're the drug that keeps me high
You're my rainbow in the sky
You're the joyful tears that I cry
And your love is the reason why...

Because without you there is no me
Without you there is no we
I now have joy in my life and your love is the key To make
my passion burn and set my spirit free...

It's so remarkable how you make me feel when you walk into
the room
And every time you leave I pray that you'll return soon
The beauty of your smile always makes me swoon
Because you're my sunshine - My beautiful flower in full
bloom...

Every time I close my eyes I see your face
And every time I look into your eyes I'm so amazed

Your love has touched me on so many levels and in so
many ways
No matter what, my love for you will always continue on
unfazed...

The touch of your love - I've never experienced anything
greater
You're the spice of Life - The sweetest of all flavors
The taste of your love I've come to savor
You've saved me from myself so you've become my savior...

I want you to know that your love will always live in the
deepest part of me
Because my love for you runs deeper than the oceans and sea
Our love can't be contained - It's enough to fill the whole
galaxy
And together throughout eternity - Our Love Will Always
Be...

"WHEN I'M WITH YOU"

When I'm with you - Time stands still,
I know love is real, and words can't express the joy I feel

When I'm with you - My passion burns,
For your touch I yearn, and fear is no longer a concern

When I'm with you - Everything seems so right,
The future seems so bright, because you are the light of
my life

When I'm with you - Sky's the limit,
All my love - I give it, and I can't imagine life without you
in it

When I'm with you - Love is the pursuit,
You're so stunningly cute, our love is absolute

When I'm with you - I want those moments to last forever,

I don't want them to stop ever, all things are possible when
we're together

When I'm with you - I'm filled with joyous laughter,
In you I've found what everyone is after, and nothing else
matters

When I'm with you - I need nothing more,
You're the key that opens the door, to what I've been
searching for

When I'm with you - Love is conceived,
Compassion is received, and all who see us will believe

When I'm with you - There's nothing I'd rather do,
Than give my all to you, you provide a happiness I
never knew

So for today, tomorrow and all the way through,
The Greatest moments in my life are...WHEN I'M WITH
YOU!!!

"YOU ARE WOMAN"

Crafted from the best parts of the inner man
So man is naturally attracted...The Creator's Plan
And it seems like He gave you all the best parts
With just one look you're able to tame a man's heart
Of all creation only you can captivate man's heart,
soul & mind
Because you're fine, divine and one of a kind
You Are Woman...

Between Grandmas, sisters, daughters, aunts and mothers
Mothers are the backbone to all families, grater than all others
No matter what you go through, no matter what you face
You always carry yourself with dignity, style and grace
You're the center of Life and without you Life would be gone
Because you're Mom, The Bomb and the reason Life goes on
You Are Woman...

Beauty...Power...Mystery...Perfection...
That's what I see in you...That's our connection

I'm amazed by your face and your body's every line and
curve
You're the greatest gift to man - Far more than we ever
deserved
The depths of your beauty is deeper than physical -
You blessed me Because you're Sensual, Sultry and Sexy
You Are Woman...

So strong but at the same time delicate
You're truly the present that Heaven sent
You know how to make something out of nothing
Life wouldn't be the same without your smile, laughter and
fussing
None other in creation can do what you do
And Life would be nothing without you
You Are Woman...

"WHY THE BROKEN HEART CRIES"

I know why the broken heart cries

Partly because of the manipulations, "B.S." and lies

But the main reason is knowing that you cheated

That's what broke the Heart and left

Love defeated And with that infidelity and betrayal

The Heart grows cold and begins to wail

Now lamentation is the only medication

To soothe sorrow's painful devastation

Articulating the grief is hard for mere words to express

The broken Heart's suffering, anguish and emptiness

The heart has many secrets that run far and deep

But it's plain to all why a broken Heart weeps

It's the Greed of the unsatisfied eye giving in to Lust

It's Love being killed do to unfaithfulness and broken trust

It's the unforgettable feeling of knowing you got played

And they say for those who seek revenge...DIG 2 GRAVES!!!

And once a person is all tried out

And once the broken Heart is all cried out

You look back and say "What were all the tears about???"

But only with maturity and time will you ever figure it out

The Heart is so deep...Who could ever truly know it

You never know it's true intentions until a person shows it

With a wondering eye many fall into Lust and can't control it

And they take the True Love they already had and just
blow it

The game of Love is not for the faint of heart

And because of you mine has been torn apart

So don t ask me again why the broken Heart cries You know
what you did...You Know Why

"MISUNDERSTOOD"

Everything' s done in due season
Anything' s possible if you're believing
All we need is a reason
And hopefully we won't fall off the deep end...

But it's the misunderstandings which makes us bump heads
And it's impatience which causes us to see red
Many make snap judgments because they don't understand
what was said
And in a flurry of rage someone can end up dead...

Many people won't take the time to see where others are
coming from
It's like to everyone else's feelings they're just numb
And many act without thinking which I find to be
really dumb
But if we would listen and think these misunderstandings
would have better outcomes...

Many will down another because he' s trying and you ain't
And many will disrespect another because he can do things
that you can't
That's the definition of an ignorant person, or at least that's
the picture that you paint
What people don't understand is some people are demonic
and so me saint...

The truth hurts that's why many people lie
What happens after death is unknown so most are scared
to die
And many can' t face this reality and that's why they get high
At one point we're all misunderstood in this world where
confusion is multiplied

And it don't matter whether you're from the suburbs or
the hood
And it don't matter whether you' re bad or good
We all want to live drama free if we possibly could
But one of the worst feeling in the world is being Misun-
derstood...

"NOW I UNDERSTAND"

You're far more than anything I could want - Far greater than anything I could perceive
You come through where others won't - you're the only one in this world that I need
When my life was in shambles you brought me hope
And you gave me strength from the words that you spoke
You never left me feeling cheated or defeated
And when I looked "Death" in the eyes you helped me to beat it
You helped me to grow into a better man
Before you I never knew friendship' s purpose but now I understand...

Without you I was a loser but since you've come everything has changed
Who would have thought that LOVE would come into my life and leave it rearranged
And it's that love that makes each of my days shine bright
And it's that love that makes me sleep good at night

Love Is Joy multiplied with Bliss
It can be expressed through a hug & kiss
Nothing can touch me as deeply as "LOVE" can
Before you I never knew Love's purpose but now I
understand...

You've given me life - You helped me cope
I was wrong, you were right - You've given me hope
When I was loss in sin you sent chastisement from above
I didn't like it at the time, but now I know You did it out
of love
You can be seen throughout creation, but some are slow to
believe - Why do they hesitate???
I didn't always see Your utter Goodness, but now Your Love I
fully appreciate
I thank You for Your forgiveness and for Your whole redemp-
tive plan
Heavenly Father before now I never knew Your purpose but
Now I Understand...

"HEAVENLY HOME"

When we're together I'm instantly swept away in the rapture that is you
And as our souls intertwine our hearts become one and no longer two
As I gaze into the insurmountable depths of your lovely eyes what do I see
The reflections of incomprehensible Life, Love and Beauty staring back at me
In this moment all my desires are fulfilled for I will never again be alone
Because with in our togetherness I can feel it...I have transcended to our Heavenly Home...

Your spirit has the capacity
To take me up to the heavenly's
And as I gaze upon what my eyes can't see
I can feel Your love staring back at are
In this moment all my desires are fulfilled for I will never again be alone

Because within our togetherness I can feel have transcended
to our Heavenly Home...

You rain Love - You rain Life
But I see Your rainbow in the sky
And as I gaze upon Your spectrum what do I see
The rays of Your loving light shining down on me
In this moment all my desires are fulfilled for I will never
again be alone
Because within our togetherness I can feel it...I have tran-
scended to our Heavenly Home...

Your smile has grabbed me and touched the depths of
my soul
It has filled me with joy so please never let go
And as I gaze upon Your glorious countenance what do I see
I see the face of Beauty Personified in an Angel staring back
at me
In this moment all my desires are fulfilled for I will never
again be alone
Because within our togetherness I know...I have transcended
to our heavenly Home...

"THE UGLINESS OF LUST"

Look at what you've done to me

I can't focus - My vision's blurry

You not truly loving me is such a tragedy

Now when I look at you pain is all I see

I'm no longer enthralled with your outer beauty at all

I was there for you whenever you'd call, but when I needed you most you were "A.W.O.L."

Is there hope for the forsaken

How can a world full of infidelity call it " Love Makin'"

With your cheating ways there were so many problems you were creating

And when I think about you I cry because even now my heart is breaking

I think about all the times you cheated and I'd still take
you back

And all the times you lied I wanted to believe you spoke true
facts

And every time you stole from me I just tried to breathe and
relax

But in the end it's as if you repeatedly chopped my heart up
with an axe

What I thought was love was nothing but "LUST"...NOW
I SEE

That my vision was blurred by Lust' s seduction, but now I
can focus clearly

So I no longer fall for Lust' s allure - I rebuke you - You no
longer have a hold on me

Seeing your lascivious grotesque nature I now know truly
beautiful is something you'll never be You entice the hearts of
all, promising pleasures with no fuss

Tempting everyone the same - The Wise & The Fool, The Poor
& The Rich, The Weak & Robust

In your wake you've destroyed The Wicked as well as The
Just so I rebuke You - I MUST!!!

Before it' s too late I hope all will recognize THE UGLINESS
OF LUST...

"ALONE WITH MY THOUGHTS"

My past is filled with regretful agitation
My present is filled with painful devastation
The depth of my sorrow can't be expressed through mere
articulation
The Future is my only hope to escape this evil manifestation...

Foolish, I pursued "Lust" when "Wisdom" should have been
sought
With sin I purchased shame and Death is what it brought
Hopelessness has overtaken me no matter how hard I fought
Now Pain & Regret is all I have as I sit ALONE WITH MY
THOUGHTS...

"IN THE END"

Before the age of man and the Devil's first sin Before Love &
Life's battle with Death and it's kin
And even before You let creation begin
You knew Love & Life would destroy Sin & Death...In The
End...

The Devil was the first to lie
Adam's disobedience caused all men to die
With the birth of sin Death was multiplied
And The Creator was the first to cry...

Even after tasting The Father's utter Goodness
His path for living we still forsook it
So we got off his straight path and took the one that's crooked
And continued to sin as if He'd overlook it...

If we would only repent, trust and believe
All of His wonderful gifts we would receive
All who bear His yoke live in ease

And the depths of His Love our finite minds can't perceive...

Like Abraham's example we should simply trust
Because with our heavenly Father obedience is a must
He's the source of our life yet we rebel and fuss
And with sinful hearts we give into Greed & Lust...

The father sacrificed His Son so forgiveness could begin
We're here today because His Love won't change, break
or bend
It's up to us to repent and obey or burn with The Judgement
of Sin
Because Love & Life will destroy Sin & Death...In The End...

"MAN'S SEARCH FOR MEANING"

Man's Search For Meaning
When you look at the world what are you seeing
What's your reason for even breathin'
I guess we all need something to believe in...

I've searched long, far and wide
I've bumped heads with the wicked and with the righteous I
collide
Until I rid myself of selfishness, vanity and pride
That was the only way I could let You get inside...

I was a fool that's all I can say
Because what I searched for I always fought and
pushed away
I was scared to accept you whenever You would come
my way
Scared of being vulnerable, and being hurt was a price I
didn't want to pay...

How could You be so close and abundant yet so
unattainable???
Many times I'd grasp at You but because of my insecurities I'd
let You go
I should have just let You run your course and go with
the flow
How could I have ever doubted You??? I just don't know...

But now that I've found You I'll always be believing
Now everywhere I look You're all I'm seeing
Now I know why I'm still breathing
Because "LOVE" is the answer to Man's Search For Meaning...

"THE DEPTHS OF DESPAIR"

In the depths of despair

You suddenly become aware

That this might be your last breath

But what comes after Death???

That's the mystery of all mysteries

But if you figure it out you could rewrite history

Because Death takes and takes

And unparalleled panic is what it creates

It takes courage to overcome it's power

But it's normal to fear Death's Hour

So live for today because there's no promise of tomorrow

And know that Love has more power than Pain & Sorrow

Because Death is a part of Life, but always know that I care

My love will always be there...Even through the Depths Of Your Despair...

"LOVE"

Love is such a beautiful deep thing

But love without you has no meaning It's like a song with no singing Like a heart with no beating

Like emotions with no feelings

Like hope without believing

Like believing you have the truth but it's really lying

Like living outside but inside you're dying

I'm a slave to your love that doesn't need freeing

I'm blind to everything else because your love is all I'm seeing

Love cuts deep but you never left me bleeding

Love is forgiveness that can keep the broken heart from seething

Killing me softly, Love's got me falling

So full of Joy, and at other times balling

When loss tears are falling, but when found always smiling

Oxymoron - Your love has me so happy that I'm crying

Because love is strong like "Popeye & Spinach"

And I can't imagine love without you in it

Because love is the ultimate prize and everyone wants to win it

And Love could change the world if everyone would just give it...

"DREAMIN'"

I didn't believe my eyes when you came into my vision
Now making you mine is my one life's mission
If loving you is work than I love my job
But you're so beautiful you have to be a mirage With perfect
harmony, Baby can't you see
I need your love - You bring out the best in me But is it
fantasy or is it reality??
Things ain't always what they seem, but I want to believe
Because you're picture perfect and that's all I know
With a body that's colder than an Alaskan Eskimo
Just promise me that we'll never say good-byes
But I know that I'm dreaming because I can't believe my
eyes...DREAMIN'...

Baby lets come together
Today is the start of our forever
I never thought I would feel this way
I never thought you would feel the same
Am I Dreamin'???

Because I can't believe what I'm seein' - You've got me feenin'
But I know this is for real
Because when I saw you our destiny was sealed
I'm tryin', I'm tryin'...I swear I'll try
To love you everyday of your life
Just promise me that we'll never say good-byes
But I know that I'm dreaming because I can't believe my
eyes...Dreamin'...

Baby if you're for real Please show me how you feel
I remember my dreams in the past
And that's when I saw you last
But now that my eyes are open
I know you're real and not just thoughts that I've chosen
Maybe you've always been there waitin'
for me to find you, totally patient
Just promise me that we'll never say good-byes
But I know that I'm dreaming because I can't believe my eyes
They say seeing is believing but for me that's not enough
Because I won't believe my eyes until I feel your
touch...Dreamin'...

"MY BRIGHT SHINING STAR"

When I look at the night's sky what do I see
I see your Bright Star shining down on me

And you shine so bright - You give my life light
With unbelievable joy - You take me to new heights

And when times get tough and it seems no one cares
It feels good to look to the sky and know you're always there

Because you' re my lucky star - Shining from afar
So beyond just par - You always raise the bar

And you opened Heaven' s Door - What more could I ask for
I asked for Love - You gave more - Because from you love
seems to pour

So Bravo - I applaud you
Many stars shine, but none quite like you

In every aspect of the word you' re remarkable
And even with clouds in the sky you still sparkle though

Because you're spectacular beyond comp are
And no matter how hard I try not to, I can't help but stare

Don' t you know that my love for you goes beyond all
comprehension
I never knew what "True Beauty" was until I watched you
with undivided attention

And I've confessed my love for you to any and all who would
listen
Now to be at one with you is my one and only life's mission

So now I travel beyond the Milky Way, beyond distant
galaxies no matter how far
Just to be with you... My Bright Shining Star...

"THE NIGHTMARE"

Dear heavenly Father - Tell me what to do
I'm having nightmares at night - Wake to find they came true
Because I've shed countless tears over the years
And all my pleas for help fell on deaf ears
I have so many questions and I looked to You for the answers
Like why does " A.I.D.S." exist and all these different forms of
Cancer???
I guess you can't have sunshine without rain
I guess you can't have joy without pain
It's The "Ying- Yang" Theory - Classified under U.F.O.
What's the purpose of this Life?? Does anybody know???
So I rack my brain, but no answers do I find
They say no one' s perfect, so was GOD flawed in our
design???
And I wonder why because of Adam's sin all of mankind
must die
And live in the nightmare of a satanic world and that is why I
cry...The Nightmare...

The nightmare...Don't Get Caught Sleepin'!!!
The Devil's so cunning with his clever schemin'
He'll break you down mentally - Have you pulling out your
own hair and screamin'
And people will say that boy's crazy not knowing that he was
possessed by a demon
Another massacre on the news - This is our reality
Another nightmare played out for the while world to see
So I pinched myself in hopes that it was just another bad
dream for me
But as soon as I felt the pain I knew there was no escaping
this tragedy
So I cover my mouth and wipe my tears in total shock
It's a shame that we can' t even sleep easy with all of our
windows and doors locked
On the 10 o' clock news countless others died from gunshots
And it's left my heart and mind numb wondering when it
will all stop
And I wonder why because of Adam's sin all of mankind
must die
And live in the nightmare of a satanic world and that is why I
cry...The Nightmare...

Now I'm at the point to where I' m scared to close my eyes
Because my dreams are filled with destruction, terror, dead
bodies and flies
From my lack of sleep I'm left paranoid, thinking everything's
a lie
Next come the hallucinations like an " LSD" High
So I've loss my grip on reality but no one seems to care
That I've totally tripped out and I'm seeing things that ain't
really there
I didn't want to face my dreams, but now it's even worse

Because I'm seeing little green men and my brain feels like It's gonna burst
My eyes are bloodshot red - I'm hearing voices in my head
I'm seeing people that are dead - "There's no escape!!" is what they said I've got to get away - This is crazy...Insane!!!
Then Hell fire came and I was burning in the flames
So I scream out in pain as the dead taunt and stare
Then I wake up to find that it was all just a nightmare...The Nightmare...

"LISTEN"

Life without GOD is a lonely highway

It's a life filled with darkness even during the day

And without Divine Guidance and His perfect plan

How can one grow spiritually and become a better man

Have you ever wondered how all of creation could be made with such precision

GOD has all the answers, but most are too busy with life to even listen

The very essence of GOD is infinite LOVE that He wants us to receive

How could anyone look at the seas, stars and the trees yet still not believe

Father GOD You saved me from myself that's why I'll always love You

Your utter Goodness is something I wish everyone knew

Still many choose to turn their backs on the truth To their own soul's destruction which none can refute

Because the road to destruction is VERY WIDE

And it looks like a party, but it's where the demons reside

Yet many choose the dark roads of lost souls

Not knowing that it leads to "Death", "Destruction" and Satanic control

In the end it's a choice between "Death" & "Life"

Will you walk in darkness or come into the light

It's true one day the student must teach

So listen to the Word as I end this sermon That I just preached

GOD is trying to save your life and your soul...That's His Mission!!!

He's been calling you, but you have to just stop and Listen...LISTEN...

"THE NARROW ROAD"

In a world full of dark roads

It's easy to come across dark souls

And with so many forks in the road

Which way are we supposed to go

One way leads to Heaven and the other to Hell

It's a test that all without Divine Guidance will fail

The road to Hell Is vast, far and wide

And dark angels make it seem like a party until they get you inside

They make it seem pleasant but it's final destination is something they hide

And you're already In Hell before you figure out that they lied

I on the other hand chose the narrow road which is rough, steep and stony

It's a road of struggle, persecution and even my loved ones act like they don't know me

Everyday I fight to stay on the narrow road knowing the Devil doesn't want me to make it

But I'm filled with the Holy Spirit so no matter what the Devil throws at me I can take it

And though you slay my flesh my spirit lives on -You can't break it

You're filled with hate with no faith while I'm saved - I know you hate it

So my friend the narrow road may not be a manicured lawn that's mowed

But In the end it leads to eternal life and streets paved with gold

Yet most still choose the easy road, fooled by It's comfort and the way it glowed

Not knowing It's the glow of Hell Fire burning up the Lost Souls

I hope in your heart grows some of the spiritual seeds that I've sowed

So listen to me and The Prophets Of Old...CHOOSE THE NARROW ROAD!!!

"TRUE LOVE"

When you're loving me you take me to the Heavenly's
True love, there's no other place I'd rather be When you're
loving me I pray this time never ended
Because True Love takes me to a state of Transcendence
True Love leaves many blinded, but now I can truly see
That you're The Angel that GOD has sent to me
To unlock the secrets of how LOVE is supposed to be
Which is the doorway to Heaven and GOD's presence
eternally
With an "Agape" nature you've descended from Heaven
above
You're better than the BEST!!! You're TRUE LOVE...

Things aren't always what they seem
And when disappointed some people scream
But you make me want to sing
With all the joy that you bring
And with you on my team
You've brought elation to the core of my being

You light up my life like sunbeams
Because you're the fulfillment of my Greatest hopes and
dreams
That's why I hold you in the highest esteem
Perfect Joy, Peace & Harmony...That's what True Love
means...

"THE HEART OF YOU"

The way you make me feel simple words can't say Your love
Is the answer to all the prayers I pray
I love you In every way
I love you more everyday...

At night when I dream It's always your face I see
Even when we're apart my mind stays on you constantly
I would describe you In four words...Love - Lover - Loving -
Lovely
I can only hope that you would use the same words to
describe me...

Though condemned and living In the Shadow of Death in the
bowls of the abyss
You've overflowed me with love and filled me with Bliss
Because of you pain & sorrow in my life doesn't exist
We connect deeper than the physical heart & mind because
together our souls inter-twist...

Now with our souls intertwined we have a bond that none
can sever
I get lost in your eyes and I could look at your smile forever
You are the culmination of Love, Joy, Peace & Perfection
brought together
And I'm left with one big question...CAN HEAVEN BE
BETTER??!!

You are my sunshine and moonlight too
Nothing can move me quite like you do
What's the meaning of LOVE??? I never had a clue
But I've found the answers all within The Heart Of You...

"A THIN LINE..."

There's a thin line between Love & Hate
There's a thin line between Reality & Fate

There's a thin line between Right & Left
There's a thin line between Life & Death

There's a thin line between Right & Wrong
There's a thin line between Flesh & Bone

There's a thin line between Today & Tomorrow There's a thin
line between Joy & Sorrow

There's a thin line between Sane & Insanity
There's a thin line between you Liking or being Mad at me

There's a thin line between Silence & Sound
There's a thin line between Feeling Up or Feeling Down

There's a thin line between Could & Can't

There's a thin line between Demonic & Saint

There's a thin line between The Foolish & The Wise
There's a thin line between Second Place & The Prize...

Epilogue :
Life Is all about choices...And if you don't know now
you know
So choose wisely because that's crucial to how your life
will go
And with these choices the Creator has been testing us since
the beginning of time
Will you pass the test knowing that Heaven & Hell are sepa-
rated by such a thin line???

"WHAT IF???"

What if Michael Jackson couldn't sing
What if dreamers couldn't dream
What if Quarterbacks had no team
What if swingers couldn't swing???

What if lemons weren't sour
What if time had no seconds, minutes or hours
What if carnivores couldn't devour
What if money had no power???

What if the sun had no light
What if Muhammad Ali couldn't fight
What if the eye had no sight
What if there was no way to make a wrong right???

What if you fed a baby with no bib
What if Eve wasn't made from Adam's rib
What If Life couldn't live
What if generosity couldn't give???

What if you worked and never got paid
What if Love would always fade
What if at creation nothing was made
What if at the resurrection Jesus stayed???

Epilogue :
There's so many things we take for granted — So many
things we don't appreciate
But if you take away even one of Life's pieces It would
change everyone's fate
Because most go through life without a single care
But if your freedom leaves you most would be devastated It's
not there
I hope as you go through life you realize that all you have is a
GOD given gift
And when you begin to take life for granted think of this
poem..."WHAT IF???"

"THIS REALITY OF SORROW"

Love is a mystery to me because I can't seem to find it
I guess living In the darkness of sorrow for so long has left
me blinded I didn't realize it before but now there's no
denying it
That my drowning in this reality of sorrow...The Devil was
behind it...

There's been countless tears shed over broken hearts
Countless tears shed from lives torn apart
Most are praying for a brand new start
But most won't come Into the light because their deeds are
dark...

No one want to be exposed to open shame
Slapping your own thigh wondering why you did those
wicked thangs
So you pray for a better day hoping things will change
But no matter what you do you can't escape the pain...

The specter of Death is filled with bliss
When he fills your life with fear, sorrow and emptiness
He hovers over us all leading some to madness
Especially when you see your name on his list...

And this nightmare that you're living in
Is because of all your sins
But you won't break and you won't bend
Until GOD helps your broken heart to mend...

The wages of sin is death...Such a hard pill to swallow
If you could do it all over again would you sin again
knowing death would follow
With yesterdays sadness, today's madness, and the terror of
Judgment Day possibly tomorrow
It's hard for you to breath while drowning In this reality of
sorrow...

"LORD KNOWS"

LORD KNOWS...I've tried to be a better man

LORD KNOWS...I always do the best I can

LORD KNOWS...I long to see a better day

LORD KNOWS...Only He can show me the way

LORD KNOWS...I'm sorry for the wrong I've done

LORD KNOWS...I'm thankful that He sent His Son

LORD KNOWS...The countless tears I've cried

LORD KNOWS...Why one day we must die

LORD KNOWS...I've cried so much throughout the years

LORD KNOWS...I need Him to wipe away my tears

LORD KNOWS...We all reap what we sow

LORD KNOWS...The heart is where His Love can grow

LORD KNOWS...Hope is where His Spirit lives

LORD KNOWS...Peace is what His Spirit gives

LORD KNOWS...The pain that I hold inside

LORD KNOWS...All the secrets that I try to hide

LORD KNOWS...Deception is the key to the Devil's power

LORD KNOWS...The Father is my Shield and Tower

LORD KNOWS...We as people can't help ourselves

LORD KNOWS...Only He can save but no one else

LORD KNOWS...What lives in the heart of man

LORD KNOWS...He's the only one who understands

LORD KNOWS...Why I hurt like this

LORD KNOWS...Why He made pain exist

LORD KNOWS...The agony I'm going through

LORD KNOWS...I can't make it without YOU

LORD KNOWS...About rain & sunshine

LORD KNOWS...Life is a mountain we must climb

LORD KNOWS...One day we'll be together

LORD KNOWS...About eternity & Forever

LORD KNOWS...My heart is pure so I don't grieve

LORD KNOWS...The whole world has been deceived

LORD KNOWS...He has blessings that we're not ready to receive

LORD KNOWS...When He comes all will believe...

"WHAT THE CREATOR'S LOVE INTENDED"

Every time I look at you I'm so amazed
And this joyful feeling goes on for days

There's no greater feeling than being with you
I'll climb the highest mountain and go through the fire
for you

There's nothing I wouldn't do to be by your side
And when you said that you loved me tears of joy is what I
cried

I'm lost in love when I'm wrapped in your arms Baby you're
the bomb so let me sound the alarms

I'm still in awe trying to figure out how you could be so
beautiful
You're Heaven in human form- How did GOD let you go

Truth is I never thought love was real

But then you came along and changed how I feel

Now you've become my only want and all I need
And filled me with emotions that before I could never have perceived

Your smile fills me with passion and joyous laughter
And I know it's love- The very thing that everyone is after

Pleasures forevermore is what you bring to my life
It's the greatest pleasure to be able to kiss and hold you at night

Only you could take my broken heart and mend it
Because you're the product that The Creator's Love Intended...

"HAPPY VALENTINE'S DAY"

Candy gets eaten, Flowers wither and cards get thrown away
But this Valentine's Day and throughout all time my love is
here to stay

So this Valentine's Day I want you to know I'll never leave
you forsaken
Because Valentine's Day is about relationships not just about
relations

This Valentine's Day I want you to know that you are my
Special One
Forget the arrow, I'm head over heels, Cupid shot me with
a gun

For Valentine's Day forget the gifts because all I want is you
On this special day I have to say it's your Love that I pursue

Valentine's Day is a time to let our love shine and if you take
a chance

You'll find out what our love can do on this day of True
Romance

Valentine's Day - Oh how I love you - Let me count the ways
One - I love you, Two I adore you - & Three - I hope you feel
the same way

Valentine's Day - Your love is the bomb - You know you stole
my heart
And I know this real - From how I feel - Not even "Death" can
keep us apart

So this Valentine's Day I want to give you a gift that will last
for all time
I give you my body - my heart - my soul - my love - and
my mind

Valentine's Day is the day we celebrate our love with
compassion
So let's make a memory of our love and our burning
passion

Valentine's Day - What more can I say - I'm glad your in
my life
I'll sacrifice more than Jesus Christ - Our love is deeper than
husband & wife

So this Valentine's Day I choose you because you're one of
a kind
I just hope you feel the same way and forever you choose to
be mine

Because if you let me - Forever I'm yours - There's nothing
left to say

Except I'll love you from now on - HAPPY VALENTINE'S
DAY!!!

"ONLY YOU CAN"

I love you and I Know you feel the same
I need you to help me end this pain
Because without you I'm stuck outside in the rain
Time reveals all things but without Love things will never
change...

Sometimes I ask myself without Love where would we be
And if there's no Heaven where do we spend eternity
Since the beginning of time our heavenly Father has said,"Just
believe in Me."
And when I look at His creation beauty is all I see...

Sometimes I wonder really what's the whole point of life Is it
just family with kids, a husband and a wife
Being born into sin so it's for our very souls we must fight
But we have a Savior beckoning us to come into The Light...

I have so many questions - So many things left unexplained
And I'm so confused - And because of my sins

I'm filled with shame
Life is filled mysteries - It's as if GOD is playing mind games
Heavenly Father what do You really want - This weighs
heavy on my brain...

Well Heavenly Father I know Your ways and thoughts are
higher than man
You know all things so I know You have a plan
In man's finite minds we couldn't possibly understand
Because we as men can't save ourselves...ONLY YOU CAN...

"LIFE'S LONELY HIGHWAY"

In this world of woe Love is hard to find
Because it's easy to hate but it's just as easy to be kind
I have so many questions that boggle my mind
Time reveals all things so I hope to have answers in due
time...

I spend each morning in pain, each afternoon in torment and
each night in sorrow
But I still try to do my best today knowing there's no promise
of tomorrow
So I pray each day for a clear path to follow
But the only thing certain in life is Death which is such a hard
pill to swallow...

And living in the shadow of Death can turn any man's heart
Into stone
In this place of bitterness it can make you feel like you're in
The Twilight Zone
It's a place of wrath, fire, & brimstone

It's like by all my loved ones I've been forsaken and by GOD disowned...

So I guess I'm the "Bad Seed"
And I'm the reason why The Messiah had to bleed
Because the preachers tried to warn me but I never took heed
So I fell into Lust, Pride & Greed...

Sin abounds — Clearly not what The Creator Intended
So many broken hearts and only He can mend it
Because sin has us all suffering and only He can end it
And take us to a better state — A state of transcendence...

If He could do it all over again would The Creator have kept sin at bay
Would he have kept Satan out of The Garden on that pivotal day
Sin's price is so steep, and Death is the price we must pay
Because sin separates us from The Creator...Leaving us on Life's Lonely Highway...

"THE WAYS OF THE WORLD"

I've fallen down, I've made many mistakes
At times I bend, but I will not break

I've been searching and searching for You
Because without You I have no one else to turn to

With no place to run and no place to hide
The truth hurts so much and that's why I lied

Please forgive my weakness, because I'm the lowest form
of man
And the pain of my plight only The Heavenly Father can
understand

Just like Adam I fell into sin
Death is the penalty, but is that the end???

So I searched The Scriptures to see what the future has In
store

Hoping when my time comes I can enter Heaven's Door

I had a great revelation after reading The Book of Revelations
On the news I see warring nations - We're on the brink of The
Great Tribulation

Is it fair that we are all born into sin and this damnable curse
Things are bad now but soon It's going to get far worse

So turn your back on the Devil, sin and evil because they will
just hurt you
But our Heavenly Father Is "LOVE" and He will never
desert you

So now the time has come to sound the alarms
Because only by faith can we make it through "Tribulation's
Storms"

So keep carrying on and try to stay strong
Because The Savior will come before too long

But to enter His Kingdom you must be as humble as a child -
A little boy or girl
And give your all to The Father and rebuke THE WAYS OF
THE WORLD...

"YOUR SOUL OR MINE"

I'm locked out of Heaven, it's Winter and It's cold outside
I'm full of self hatred being a born sinner with no place
to hide

So I pray for forgiveness and look to GOD for an answer
In hopes that He will remove all sin which is deadlier than
Cancer

I know In the end the Devil can't win
Hatred produces sin, but GOD's love will bring sin to en end

But I look at my past and all of the mistakes I've made
Over time my heart grew cold and my love for others seemed
to fade

The realist of the real is one day you're going to die and leave
all this "B.S." behind you
Heavenly Father I've looked for You everywhere - IS DEATH
THE ONLY WAY TO FIND YOU??!!

So I dropped to my knees and hoped that GOD would forgive my scheming
And help me clean out my closet and rebuke all these demons

I'm so ashamed because I'm a sinner in the worst degree
I'm so deep in the wrong that Your forgiveness is hard for me to see

My life of stress is so taxing
Because I'm going through Hell where there's no relaxing

I long for love but the thing that's strange
Is how hate has made my prospective rearrange

But "LOVE" You didn't change, I'm the one who changed
Love why can't You see You were my everything

I contemplate on man's fallen state...This was not GOD's original design
So examine yourself because on Judgment Day it'll either be YOUR SOUL OR MINE...

"THE SANDMAN"

I made a deal with The Sandman to make my dreams come true
I sold my soul to The Sandman so that I'll always dream of you
Because it's your love that I pursue
But the sad thing is you never knew
That when I look at you
In that moment my dreams came true...

But there's always a catch in The Sandman's land of fantasy
Although the dreams may be vivid they'll never really be reality
And when we kiss it's not really you that's having me
So it doesn't take long to figure out it's not really you that I see
Now I want out of this dream which is a total catastrophe
But to get here I signed a deal in blood so now there's no saving me...

I thought you could make my dreams come true but you had
another plan
I thought you really cared but now I know you never gave
a damn
You said you could grant my dream wishes if I'd only take
your hand
Some say be careful what you wish for, you just might get
it....Now I understand
Because life's not meant to be all cotton candy, rainbows, and
walks on the sand
But by the time I figured that out I'd already lost my soul to
The Sandman...

"JOY & PAIN - HATE & LOVE"

JOY...
Joy is the experience of effervescent bliss It's felt whenever we're hugged or kissed
It's the wonderful feeling when you're reunited with someone you've missed
JOY...There's no greater feeling than this... JOY...

PAIN...
Pain is crippling and exceedingly bad
It's the opposite of JOY, leaving you perpetually sad
It brings Destruction & Death - Enough to drive the strongest man mad
PAIN...It leaves all in Agony with the worst feeling you've ever had... PAIN...

HATE...
Hate fuels the fire of Wrath
It consumes & destroys all who enter it's path It's the ultimate enemy of LOVE - It's a sociopath

HATE...It benefits no one - It's utterly worthless - It's A
Psychopath... HATE...

LOVE...
Love is complete happiness that never will stall
It's pleasures forevermore that never falters, fails or falls
Against all it's enemies it stands tall
LOVE...It's in all, is all and conquers all... LOVE...

"LOVE PURIFIED"

I want to be the one who keeps you warm when it rains
And if need be I'll be the one who will take away all your
pains

I breathe for you
And if need be I'll bleed for you

I'll never leave you
Because I believe in you

You fill me with a joy I never knew
And when you smile I hope it's because you feel the same
way too

I want you to know that I'm down for you
And there's nothing I wouldn't do

To give the world to you
And you deserve it too

I've spent many years of my life looking for love but every-
where I've searched
I'd end up broken down, torn up and hurt

Until I came across you and you turned my life inside out
So you took away all my fears & pain, and showed me what
love is all about

You put an end to all my secrets and lies
Because in the face of "True Love" there's no need to hide

The greatest feeling in the world was the moment I let you
inside
You're Truth, You're Mercy, You're Bliss...You're LOVE
PURIFIED...

"BABY PLEASE COME HOME"

I just can't forget you
LORD knows I've tried to It took a lifetime to find you
But your love left me deaf, dumb and blind too
So when you left I was completely blind sided
And this overwhelming feeling of loneliness I couldn't fight it
It cut me to the bone
Because I can't move on I'm not that strong
Baby please come home...

By myself at night I cry
Thinking about you and I
And everything that's went wrong
Since you've been gone
The pain has grown
Because I'm all alone It's cut me to the bone Because I can't
move on I'm not that strong
Baby please come home...

Now when I smile it's a lie

A front so that people won't see me cry
But that fake smile can't hide
That without you I'm broken inside
Now I have no one to turn to- No one in which to confide
And when you walked out of my life the love in me slowly
died It's cut me to the bone
Because I can't move on I'm not that strong
BABY PLEASE COME HOME!!!

"A LOVE POEM"

Beyond the horizon I see your face
And I'm lifted beyond reality, time and space
You make my heart speed up it's pace
Now in my life sorrow no longer has a place...

Over every aspect of my life you take precedence With a
smile that's OH SO heaven sent
All your attributes I find to be magnificent
That's why to leave your side I'm hesitant...

Now I find myself caught in the rapture of you
The grass seems greener and the sky is bluer than blue
I love your laughter and your spirit too
You've brought peace to my soul which I thought no one
could do...

This is real love purified
I know it's real because of how I feel inside
And it's a feeling that can't be denied

My love for you is something I just can't hide...

With each passing second my love for you grows How did
you get so beautiful - Only GOD knows
In the past I've been hurt so my heart turned cold- It
FROZE!!!
Sometimes you love and lose- That's just how it goes...

I can't promise that there will always be sunny weather I've
learned a long time ago to never say never
But I promise to stay true to you forever
Just promise me we'll always be together...

This is how I truly feel, but you never knew
That's why I wrote this Love Poem just for you...

"LOVE PERSONIFIED"

Over the ages I've crossed oceans of time
To find a love like yours which is one of a kind...

And even though you're not here with me now I've got to
make you mine some way some how...

From dusk to dawn you are my moon light
And from dawn to dusk you bring light to my life...

In times of sorrow you help me cope
And when times get tough you bring me hope...

Is it destiny or is it GOD's plan
For you to bring out the best of me and help me stand???

It's so remarkable how you make me feel
Because my heart was so damaged but you helped me heal...

A lifetime with you would not be enough

Because I want to spend all of eternity within your touch...

You make me wish for more hours in a day
To express how you make me feel I can't quite find the words
to say...

All I can say is you make me feel brand new
And there's nothing greater in existence than finding a love
that's true...

And I've found in you a joy that only True Love could bring
Your love is the fulfillment of my only wish and my greatest
dream...

Sad but true, most go through life and never experience the
exquisiteness
Of the passionate fire that burns within your kiss...

And it's taken so long but I'm glad that I waited
To find love in human form, to find Love Incarnated...

I now know you're what everyone's searching for but in the
end you can't hide
Because You're Beautiful, You're Divine, You're Love
Personified...

"THIS GOOD-BYE"

You broke my heart

Now my days are dark And this is insane

I can't escape this pain

And it's raining outside but these tears I can't hide

I'm drowning in sorrow Don't wanna face tomorrow

Each day is a curse

Yesterday was bad, but today is even worse Within my heart misery has taken up residence

And on my mind the memory of your betrayal takes precedence

Why did you cheat - Why did you lie???

And you did it all while looking me straight in the eye

If you didn't want me why didn't you just leave???

Because you already knew lying & cheating were my biggest pet peeves

So I tried to drink my pain away

But it seems like the pain was here to stay

My nights are filled with anguish and shame fills my day

And wishing to forget you is the only prayer I pray

Because I can't handle the memories - NO!!! Not this time

Who would have thought Love & Hate would have such a thin line???

You were my sunshine, but now I'm in the rain

I was true to you...Why couldn't you do the same???

Sad but true, I still love you

But you shattered my heart and me with a pain I never knew

You've left a hole in my heart, a void in my life, and a tear in my eye

I would say good-bye, but there's nothing good about This Good-Bye...

"I'M JUST VENTING" (AN INTERLUDE)

From L.A., to New York, to New Orleans Hot sauce, corn
bread and collard greens

I'm here to kill your dreams and take your position
Cancerous to your health and without remission

I hope you're paying attention, I'll make your fate worse than
prison
Because I'm a star in this name, and the captain said pick him

Another victim - I'll get em', If I see wigs I will spit em'
If I see dollars I spend em', If I see hoes I will pimp em'

I'm on a f*cking war path, and ain't no stopping this anger
A mind f*cked individual, I guess I'm hooked on this danger

Because I'm a restless bullet, can't wait to leave the damn
chamber
I got a one-eyed homie, compared to me he's much stranger

I make the world go round, and people chase me like money
Because I'm starving for freedom, but you ain't never been
hungry

Until you've been in my shoes, beat down-broke-and abused
Locked in a cell - "Human Zoos", I think I left GOD confused

So what's left in the plan, I'm just a shell of a man It's like I'm
buried in sand, How much pain can one stand

Because I just might explode, and then lose all control
But that was never my goal, tell me why tears always flow???

But they're the tears of a clown, because the joke was on me
I think you have to no blind before you truly can see

How the pain gets worse, I think we've all been cursed
Welcome to the sorrow of my "Three Pound Universe..."

I'm Just Venting...

"UTTERLY BEAUTIFUL"

My love for you is unending - It transcends time You make
me feel like I'm winning - You blow my mind
You're so brilliant - Nothing can dull your shine
And for someone to not appreciate your beauty they would
have to be blind...

You bring joy to my life like cotton candy & rainbows
You're fine and refined from your head to your toes
You ooze sweetness and from you joy flows
Eyes can be deceived, but this is LOVE and my heart knows...

I can't quite put my finger on it, is it your sensuality?
Or is it your stunning smile that's stabbing me??
Maybe it's your cool personality that's grabbing me
It really doesn't matter, I'm just glad that in your life you're
having me...

You're the epitome of glamorous - It's in your eyes You're so
alluring - Your heart is the prize

Because you have the biggest heart, but not measured by physical size
It's your heart's purity that get out of me the biggest rise...

It's the little things like the way you walk that entices me
And every time you smile it's so exciting to me
Because me finding you has always been my destiny
It's like the cosmos and stars have been guiding you to me...

When I was in need of love you were there to lend it
Your love's the greatest prize in creation and I want to win it
Whenever you're away I count down the seconds and minutes
Now I can't imagine my life without you in it...

Because you're my Angel - I see your halo
Like the stars you glow - But you didn't even know So hold me tight and don't ever let go
There's only two words that describe you..."Utterly Beautiful..."

"LOVE AT FIRST SIGHT"

From the first moment you blessed my eyes with the sight
of you
My heart melted, my soul quacked and I instantly knew
That I loved you and this is true
And this is something that only your presence could do...

I never thought it would happen and I don't believe my eyes
But this feeling that I'm feeling is LOVE recognized
You now have my heart, I'll tell you no lies
I'm crying out for your affection...Don't you hear my sighs???

I think we were destiny or better yet it's our fate
I know you were meant to be my one and only mate
Before my eyes met yours I was bitter and filled with HATE
But now the thought of you not, loving me is more than I can
take...

Now that I've seen your face
All my sorrows have been erased

I always wondered how love would taste
There's no other in creation that could take your place...

Now it seems everywhere I look it's your face I see
And from the moment I saw you I knew we were meant to be
I'll give you my heart- My all, because your love is the key
To the ultimate goal- To our destiny...

So please be mine I promise I'll treat you right I'll make you smile and be the light of your life

And the way you make me feel is a feeling I can't fight

Because when my eyes met yours it was Love At First Sight...

"A KISS BEFORE DYING"

I never thought I would never see you again I never thought
our love affair would end...

I knew you were the one I've been waiting for
But when you walked out that door it hurt me to the core...

You were the only one who could move my soul with just a
smile
So I'm trying to figure out how you could walk out of my life
now...

You were the light of my world, but now my days feel like
night
Because you're not by my side to make things go right...

When you were here I never shed a tear
To love again I fear because my heart's been seared...

All I know is you're gone, and I don't know where we went wrong
You can hear the pain in my tone - It's like you broke all my bones...

Everyone says there are a lot of fish in the sea
But you were my TRUE LOVE- A one of a kind beauty...

So now I'm drowning my pain at the bottom of alcoholic bottles
But it doesn't seem to get to the root of all my sorrows...

I MISS YOU- More than you could ever know it
Because I LOVE YOU- But never got the chance to fully show it...

I miss your spirit- I miss your laughter
And without you I'll never have my "Happily Ever After"...

You never knew that in my life you were the most important piece
And even though you're gone my love for you has never wavered or ceased...

When I think of our last kiss I'm always sighing- I'm always crying
Because it was "Love's Death Kiss"- IT WAS A KISS BEFORE DYING...

"DO YOU EVER THINK OF ME???"

The loss of your love is a pain so severe
Now my life is left in shambles without you here
It meant the world to me to be within your care
Now my house is not a home because you're no longer there
With you gone I'm experiencing_a loneliness I never knew
My mind quacks, my body aches and in my heart the
sorrow grew
You were the one I could count on when all else failed
Just knowing your love is out there shows me that HATRED
won't prevail
But the mere absence of your presence has left me devastated
You just don't know the havoc that life without you has
created
Every second we're apart feels like an eternity
I wonder if I ever cross your mind - Do You Ever Think Of
Me???

I miss the look in your eyes - I miss the feel of your touch
But it's the beauty of your heart that I miss so much

I was in awe of your smile and even your graceful walk
It'd send chills down my spine just to hear you talk
But it's so cold how you left me - Since then my world's been charming
Because you took your love and left me totally hanging
Now I'm trying to picture love without you
It's like air without oxygen - Like the sky not being blue
Because you were my one true love - My greatest dream come true
Now I don't know what to do or how to go on without you
Even when I close my eyes it's always your face that I see
But I wonder if I ever cross your mind - Do You Ever Think Of Me???

How can I carry on now that your love is gone
I'm left bitter down to my bones - Can't you hear the pain in my tone
I thought you were my friend, but now here's the lesson I've learned Don't love too hard because you might end up getting burned
Love can turn your world up side down but most are unaware
That the game of love can sometimes be played so unfair
While I had your love nothing else mattered
But now you've gone away and it's left my heart shattered
I can still feel your love and all of it's power
But you've left me so low...Like at Death's Hour
I still love you though and still hope that you'll return...Eventually
But in the mean time I still wonder - Do You Ever Think Of Me???

"AS LONG AS YOU LOVE ME"

Your love is the path to Youth's Fountain
Your love takes me higher than the highest mountain
But at the same time runs deeper than the ocean or sea
And I'll always be happy, as Long As You Love Me...

For your love I've hopelessly fallen
And your love has rescued me every time I've called Em'
You've showed me how love is supposed to be
And my heart will always flutter, As Long As You Love Me...

Your love is not a game to be played with like a toy I've found
your love to be essential to my joy
Your love has moved my soul and that anyone can see
And I can overcome anything, As Long As You Love Me...

Your love frees me from all pressures
The way you smile and hold my hand are more to me than
simple gestures Our mutual respect and trust are the key

And my heart beats for only Thee, As Long As You
Love Me…

Your love has me on top of the world
We're kindred spirits and our souls are intertwined in a
passionate swirl
You're lovely but I'm most impressed with your inner beauty
And nothing else matters, As Long As You Love Me…

All of your love's attributes would to impossible to list
Total Bliss can only be found within your arms or your kiss
You've given me a glimpse of Heaven and how it's going
to be
And my passionate fire will always burn, As Long As You
Love Me...

So come with me and never leave my side
I could be selfish, but the world needs your love so please
don't hide
Because your kind of love the world has been waiting to see
But you'll always be my everything, As Long As You Love
Me...

"YOU ARE MY FOREVER"

I wondered if love is real then GOD gave me a sign Because
He sent you to me and you blew my mind

You're a Majestic Angel sent to me from Heaven
But I know I don't deserve this Sacred Blessing

I've never felt how you've made me feel thus far
At night you shine like the moon and the stars

Your body's curves are criminal so I'm prepared to break
the law
I'm so far beyond infatuated, you have me in a state of awe

Your beauty's on my mind, all the time, you seem to shine
You're the dime of all dimes, so fine, with a spirit so refined

I trust you with my heart because I know you won't break it
And no matter what life brings I know with your love I can
take it

Whenever I'm alone with you nothing can feel more splendid
And in that moment all of my pain, sorrow and heartache
ended

When I look into your eyes my heart melts and I'm totally
enchanted
I've felt love before but it's like you've taken LOVE and
enhanced it

I've never felt love so amplified, with so much joy I almost
cried
To say LOVE is blind is a lie because you're a love that no one
could hide

You're one of a kind, I'll never leave you behind
Our love will last for all time, You're GOD's Perfect Design

And when my heart sunk low to the depths of HELL where
no one could see it Your love went through the flames to grab
my heart and retrieve it

You've lifted me up to Heaven, Peace and total serenity
And where others failed you've showed me I could depend
on Thee

Just being with you brings me the ultimate pleasure
Because you're my all, my everything...YOU ARE MY
FOREVER...

"THESE FOUR WALLS"

These Four Walls... Everyday I try to meditate
But these four walls my thoughts can't penetrate These four
walls seem to devastate
They're like one step away from HELL's Gate
I can't begin to tell you the frustration these four walls create
And you can find yourself behind them if you make a
mistake
And for many behind these four wall it's too late Because it
would take an act of GOD to change their fate
These Four Walls...

These Four Walls...
These four walls got me trapped in my own mind
A place where nothing changes but the calendar and time
A place where sorrow is the norm and joy you can't find
A place where the heart turns cold and love is left behind
Behind these four walls I've lost many years
Behind these four walls I've lost many peers Behind these

four walls I've shed countless tears Behind these four walls
I've faced my worst fears These Four Walls...

These Four Walls...
These four Walls bring pain
They trap the foolish and wise just the same
In here you're just a number with no name
And if you're not strong minded you'll go insane
When you're behind these four walls there's no place to go
It's a place where tears never cease to flow
These four walls can make anyone lose control
And if you're not careful you'll even lose your soul These
Four Walls...

"MISERY & DESPAIR"

I've been loving you for so long
How could you do me so wrong
I've run out of tears - They're all gone
Now my life is like the product of sad songs...

And sad songs say so much
miss your smell - Your smile - Your touch
And simple pleasures like sharing our lunch
But the pain of this day came to me without so much as a
hunch...

So I was totally blind-sided
How could I know your true intentions when you'd hide it
I knew you were cheating but you'd always deny it
But once I had proof our fate was decided...

My heart has been crushed - My mind has exploded
The pain is so deep and I can't control it
How could you set me on fire and I don't even know it

To think I gave you my heart and into the trash is where you throw it...

I should have known better, but what I thought was "LOVE" blinded me
And I didn't want to believe that all you did was lie to me...

I wanted to believe that love conquers all
But in a one-way love the lover's heart will fall Then love turns to hate with your fist in a ball
You end up talking to yourself and screaming at the walls...

The pain has you insane but it's only because you care
And you feel so alone because they're no longer there
So you have to let go - I wrote this to make you aware
That Misery loves company, but so does Despair...

"I LOVE YOU"

When I think of you the sun shines brighter
And when I look at you, you take me higher
There's no greater sensation than your loving touch
Just knowing you believe in me means so much Knowing you
has been the ultimate blessing
Because you don't play games or keep me guessing I love you
because you keep it real
I love you because total elation is how you make me feel
I love you and this is a fact that can't be ignored
And because I love you I'll give my life in exchange for yours
I LOVE YOU...

Everyday I spend with you you give me everything I'm
looking for
And as we pass the test of time I realize you're everything I
need and more
I'm lost in your love and I want to kiss you forever
Because when we're together nothing could be better

Only two words can describe your smile...Breathtaking &
Remarkable
And when us two are together our love is absolutely
unstoppable
I love you because of your inner beauty
I love you because your spirit moves me
I love you for loving me which is only logical
But mostly I love you because you've shown me True Love is
possible I LOVE YOU...

"FOR OH SO LONG"

For oh so long I've long to find A love that would combine
Bliss and Joy whenever
Me and You come together
So promise me your hand from now on
Because I've waited for this moment...For Oh So Long

For oh so long I've been endlessly searching
To find a love like yours to end my heart's hurting
For without your love pain was the only thing that was
certain
And to end my pain a kiss From you is the only thing that's
working
Your beauty is so inspiring I could write you a million love
poems
So on bended knee I've wanted to tell you I love you...For Oh
So Long

For oh so long I've journeyed through life
Living in darkness in search of light

Until I came across your love which was my savior And you cleansed my soul and corrected my behavior
So I show you love through obedience and I praise You through song
Heavenly Father, all of creation has been waiting to meet You...For Oh So Long

For oh so long I've been looking for my better half
Someone who I can trust, who takes me serious but can also make me laugh
Someone who can stand the test of time and will always treat me right
Someone who wants to be with me forever as husband and wife
And I need that someone to be you because within you is a love so strong
And my eternal love has been burning for you...For Oh So Long...

"BETRAYAL"

Because of your betrayal

You've turned the table

Now I'm unable

To let this pain go

Revenge is so cold, but you kinda see it coming

But Betrayal is colder, because you're blind-sided by it's cunning

Betrayal did me so cold...Colder than Cancer

And you've left me saying why and looking for answers

I really thought you had my back and that you'd love me forever

But you told a multitude of lies so our bond was severed

Only the Betrayed know what I'm going through

I loved you with my all, but your love for me wasn't true

And I don't think anyone can understand the depths of my sorrows

Just to spend one day with True Love I'd give up a million tomorrows

And my anguish is so deep, but what's a damn shame

Is I wasted my love on you, but you never felt the same

How could I love you so much but your heart was never truly there

How could I feel such a deep loss when you never truly cared

You left me burning in the flames, and didn't care about my pain

There ain't no shame in your game, but I would never do you the same

You turned your back on me and left me in agony

Now pain and suffering is all I can see

Now I'm unable

To let this pain go

Because you've turned the table

And nothing hurts deeper than...BETRAYAL...

"THE LAND OF SHATTERED DREAMS"

All I ever wanted was someone who cares and will always be
there
But you turned my joys into fears and my happiness into
tears

I tried to be patient and let all the B.S. slide
But the more I waited the more I found that you were evil
inside

Before I met you I had a spirit I thought was unsinkable
But you shattered that spirit when you did the unthinkable

Like the Devil you're a rebel that GOD can't even save
But they say if one seeks revenge he needs to dig 2 graves

There's only so much a man can take Screwing me over was
your fatal mistake

I had to split your wig for the sh*t you did

I thought I knew you but you kept the real you hid

And by the time I found out you was corrupt You left my life in shambles and all torn up

How things turned out, could it be my fault because I didn't pray enough
Or could it be that when I prayed I didn't say enough

Life with you was so damn rough
My soft heart let you get away with murder when I should've been tough

Only the abused know what I went through and how I feel
Boxed in a corner - To save my life I had to kill

It wasn't Revenge or planed out - Maybe it was Fate
If I could do it all over again I would have tried harder to escape

So they gave me prison and call it Justice, Justice isn't always what it seems
Justice has failed me - I live in prison...The Land Of Shattered Dreams...

"WHENEVER I'M NEAR YOU"

When I was lost in confusion and going through life without
a plan You were the only one who cared when others didn't
give a damn
You were the only one to help me - You are the only one who
understands
And I can even cry in front of you and not feel like less of a
man...

Whenever I'm sad you always come and cheer me up
And whenever I'm sick you make me better with your
healing touch
You always come through for me in the clutch
Your heart is filled with beauty, compassion, love and things
of such...

Your beautiful smile is OH SO Heavenly
And when I first saw you I knew we were meant to be
All my life I've been lonely until the day you came to me
Now your love is my greatest fantasy brought into reality...

When my life was out of focus and I didn't think I'd make it through
You gave me strength and brought my focus back into clear view
When we're together there's nothing we can't do
You make me a better me...Whenever I'm Near You...

"WHAT LOVE CAN DO"

Love can heal all wounds - Love can transcend time
Love can mend the broken heart - Love can blow your mind

Love can cleans your soul - Love can end all pain
Love can overcome hatred - Love can make a savage
man tame

Love can move mountains - Love can turn the wise into fools
Love can change the cold-hearted - Love can use the heart as
it's tool

Love can turn a frown into a smile - Love can make a Lover's
heart flutter
Love always goes the extra mile - Love's the greatest gift we
give one another

Love is Kind - Love is Patient
Love is Gentle - Love has no Limitations

Love is Mercy - Love is Bliss
Love is the joy sometimes found within a kiss

Love is inexact - Love can be abstract
There are many emotions, but "LOVE" has the greatest impact

Love brings together husband & wife - Love takes us to new
heights
I love "LOVE" with all my might - Love is the reason why we
were given life

So look into your heart and I'm sure you'll discover
That that's where Love lives with all it's splendor & wonder

In today's world of woe the one thing I found to always
be true
Is that only "LOVE" can save us...That's What Love Can On...

"TOTAL ELATION"

Alone in this world I can't take it

But with you by my side I know I can make it

I know I couldn't have made it this far without your help

Because you mean more to me than Life itself

You give me strength

Because you're Heaven sent

So the love you send

Please don't let it end I'll never leave you

Because I need you

You're the very air I breathe

The only reason I still believe

You're the reason I continue to try

My greatest hope and only reason why

Your love lives in my heart

So we'll never be apart

I'll walk out of Heaven if you're not there

Because that's how much I love you and how deeply that
I care

With you in my life I know love is real without doubt

You've turned my life inside out and showed me what love is
all about

I only wish you knew that it's your heart that I pursue

Because loving you is all I want to do

Like rain from above

You've showered me with love

It's soul penetratin' - And put an end to my hatin'

Because I spent my whole life waitin' - For this feeling of
Total Elation...

THE WORLD OF EMOTIONS"

Joy fills all with Gladness - Sorrow is the result of Sadness
Confusion ends in Madness - Hatred brings Pain the fastest

It takes Humility, Patience & Understanding to Forgive

But to hold a Grudge it take Selfishness, Bull-headedness &
Bitterness to live

Apprehension makes one Hesitate and often ends in Regret

Envy & Desire drive some Crazy, craving things they can't get

Chaos brings a world of Disarray and opens you up to Cata-
strophe

Sin brings Terror, Calamity, Grief and separation from
GOD...The Ultimate Tragedy

Deceit is a Liar and Devious, leaving the Naive tricked

Agony has Disheartened many with the Pain and Suffering
he inflicts

With Bullying, Aggravation & Irritation, Revenge is on the horizon

But with Positivity, Discipline & Wisdom we can end needless Despising

It's good to be Ambitious, but don't forget to stay Meek

They say only the Strong survive, but it's a Gentle touch that most seek

If you ever met "Lonely" he introduces you to "Abandonment"

And he leads you to the house of Anxiety where Dismay is prevalent

Then Worry takes over and you find yourself Anxious

Because when the Awkwardness of Paranoia kicks In most can't take this

In life without Risk there's no reward

But with Inspiration Confidence can be restored And as long as you're Untroubled by Insecurity

With Determination the world can become a great place through Ingenuity

Because Success has a Charm and Allure it's own

It's a place of Cheerfulness - Such a Pleasant home

In the end there's one thing that has left me Perplexed

That even with all these Emotions the human heart hasn't been Satisfied as of yet With so many Feelings many get lost in the Commotions

But one day I Hope you'll find Contentment in The World Of Emotions...

"MY SYMPHONY"

Welcome to my symphony Where there's just you and me
Dancing to my melody
But your love is all I see...

I can hear the sweet sound
Every time you come around
So lets party and get down
While my symphony's in town...

So listen to my composition
To make you groove is my mission
There really ain't no competition
Just bounce to this while you listen...

My symphony can change the world - Now ain't that
somethin'
With vocals, rhythm & blues, rap & percussion
I always keep the party jumpin' with the beats bumpin'

There's nothing in the world quite like it - Absolutely
Nothin'...

I know I have you spellbound with the music that I make
I can tell you're fascinated by the sounds I create
The irresistible allure of my bass & treble you just can't debate
Because the exquisite sound is almost more than you can
take...

So groove to the beat of my symphony's instrumental
Because making a beautiful sound for me is fundamental
I live to do this music and the next line is not meant to be a
riddle Music is my life but after each composition I die just a
little...

With infinite styles and infinite sounds music's destined to be
the language of the world and bring you closer to me
Music's melody has a deeper meaning - A deeper beauty
to see
It's an expression of True Love - This Is My Symphony...

"RAIN"

I guess you can't have joy without pain
I guess you can't have sunshine without rain
I hear the rain (Drip-Drop, Drip-Drop) I hear the rain (Drip-Drop, Drip-Drop)

And when I feel the rain falling across my face I stick my tongue out to have a taste
I hear the rain (Drip-Drop, Drip Drop) I hear the rain (Drip-Drop, Drip-Drop)

And when you're tumbling down there's no need to rehearse
Rain is the only one who can quench the world's thirst
I hear the rain (Drip-Drop, Drip-Drop) I hear the rain (Drip-Drop, Drip-Drop)

And when I see the grey clouds in the sky
I pray for rain to come and don't pass me by
I hear the rain (Drip-Drop, Drip-Drop) I hear the rain (Drip-Drop, Drip-Drop)

On My skin I feel Rain's gentleness
And it lets me know that you were Heaven sent
I hear the rain (Drip-Drop, Drip-Drop) I hear the rain (Drip-Drop, Drip-Drop)

And I don't need no shelter from this stormy weather
So lets stay together so that it rains forever
I hear the rain (Drip-Drop, Drip-Drop) I hear the rain (Drip-Drop, Drip-Drop)

It's raining Love - It's raining life...
But there's a rainbow in the sky...

And you're never too far away
To rain your love down on me

Because we have a bond that none could sever Only GOD could put this together

You have the capacity - To bring out the best of me
And I wonder how my world would he - If you weren't here to rain on me

So let your love fall from the sky and don't ever change
Because the world just wouldn't be the same
without..."RAIN"...

"VISIONS OF YOU AT NIGHT"

At night I always dream of you
And the visions I have I wish in reality they would come true

Nights without you are always so cold
Because only you can keep me warm with the love in my
heart that you've sowed

You give me quality in quantity and overwhelm my senses
And I've been hooked on your love every since this

You're the light of my life and you shine like stars in the
night sky
Nothing can take me as high as how I feel when I look into
your eyes

I've had other lovers but none could take me there like
you do
There's no substitute for you...I'm nothing without you

Now everywhere I look I see your beautiful face
In the moon, the stars and beyond time & space

Visions of you come to me at the midnight hour
Then I lose all control...Over me you have that power

So now live for the night knowing the darker it is the brighter
you shine
And you make my dreams come true with my visions of you
at nighttime...

"LOST IN YOUR LOVE"

Lost in your love is where you'll find me
Where I put hatred, selfishness & pride far behind me
Because my passion for you burns with an unquenchable fire
So let our bodies intertwine in Love's flames of desire
And where you are is where I want to be
Because I'm lost in your love where only you can find me
Lost In Your Love...

Lost in your love but I'm so glad that I found you No other in
creation has the power to do what you do
Sweeter than honey, more precious than all jewels
And everyone longs to be in a world where your love rules
Because you're out of sight, but at the same time anyone
can see
That I'm lost in your love where only you can find me
Lost In Your Love...

Lost in your love - Please say you'll be mine
In all of creation your beauty is one of a kind

So please don't waste time, and don't leave me behind
Because your love's a treasure I never thought I'd find
So now you've got my heart on lock, but at the same time
you've set me free
And that's why I'm glad to be lost in your love where only
you can find me Lost In You Love...

Lost in your love, OH HOW SWEET THE SOUND
You're like rain from above on my heart's parched ground
And even at your worse you've never let me down
That's why I've never been the same since you've came
around
You're the realization of all my hopes & dreams - you fulfilled
my destiny
That's why I'm hopelessly lost in your love where only you
can find me Lost In Your Love...

"GLORIOUS LOVE"

Love...I love the way you love me
Love..Put no one else above me
Love...I love the way you love me
Love...I put no one else above Thee
Love...I love the way you love me
Love...I feel so unworthy
Love...I love the way you love me
Because Love...Your love is all I see...

Love...What a beautiful concept
Love...It's the present that GOD sent

Love...How could anyone doubt it
Love...I'm so happy I found it

Love...Has the gentlest embrace
Love...Has the sweetest of all taste

Love...Is more precious than all jewels

Love...Can turn the wise into blind fools

Love...Is what everyone lives for
Love...Is the path to Heaven's Door

Love...Oh how sweet the sound
Love...So glad you came around

Love...Is the combination of Beauty, infinite Joy and total satisfaction
Love...Is all your Hopes realized with Peace & Bliss as a reaction

Love...Is the light of the universe
Love...Is the cure for any curse

Love...I love the way you love me
And to be Loved is the Greatest Of All Glory...

"FATHER GOD"

Father GOD I know I fell short of Your Glory
But You're still always there to care for me And when I pray
You never did ignore me
Because You're The light, The Peace and The Hope in my life's
story...

Father GOD You sent Your Son here to take my place
To suffer sin's shame, torment and disgrace
He suffered agony no mere man could take
His sacrifice brought salvation to the whole human race...

Father GOD I wish everyone knew Ya
Because if they knew Your Goodness they would all
pursue Ya
You're infinitely wise so no one could fool Ye
I know on Judgment Day on bent knee all will say,
"Halleluyah!!!"

Father GOD only You can rule the universe as one nation

And to feel Your love is the ultimate sensation
Throughout the universe we see Your finger in all of creation
And just knowing that You want the best for us is such a
revelation...

Father GOD we all know the Devil comes to steal, kill,
destroy and rob
How could he ever think he could be on Your level and do
Your job
You're perfect in every way and how people could doubt You
is so odd
Because You're The Most High, You're The Almighty...You're
Father GOD...

"EXPRESSIONS OF LOVE"

Love is the fulfillment of everyone's ultimate desire
It's a passion that burns with un-tamable fire

It's everyone's desired destination and ultimate truth
It's an exquisite joy that none can refute

The expressions of Love are giving your all and total sacrifice
Because without love for each other there's really no point
to life

And when two unite as one in Love's tender embrace
You can look into each others eyes and see Love's face

The heart is it's symbol, but the mind is the key Love touches
the soul - Love is Heavenly

Love is filled with mercy, Kindness, Joy & Generosity
And when my heart was broken Love was the only way to
heal me

Love has the ability to move mountains and part the sea
Love is all of our hopes fulfilled - It shows us how we're
supposed to be

Love is Light - Love is a hug and not a shove
For love I'd sacrifice my life which can be the ultimate expres-
sion of Love...

"MY HEART BELONGS TO YOU"

I've fallen in love with you
As a result of the things you do
We're united as one and no longer two
Because you take me to heights I never knew...

You own a piece of me that's located in my left chest
And you cleaned up my life where before there was a mess
We belong together and that's something no one can contest
But it's your inner beauty that I find to be the best...

My heart beats for you and your passion is the energy
That lets me know Love is real - That always brings you
to me
And what I have is precious, but I give it you freely
Because I want to be at one with you in total unity...

So whatever you want I'm here to provide
You'll see I am nothing but love once I let you inside
It's like ecstasy meets euphoria when our bodies collide

And the joy that we feel could never be denied...

With you in my life I could never feel blue
You've shown me what True Love can do so my expectancy grew
They say Love conquers all, and now I know that it's true
You're my one True Love - My Heart Belongs To You...

"LIKE A STAR"

Your love's like a star I see shining
It's on top of a mountain I've been climbing

And it seems like I'll never get up there
But I keep trying so you'll know that I care

And it's so remarkable how you shine so brightly Even when
my world is dark your light still finds me

You're beautiful and that's all I can really say
You turn my frown up side down and turned my night
into day

Just like a star your body is celestial
And if I ever held you in my arms I'd never let you go

Where did you come from??? I'd say Heaven if I had to guess
Love is Light!!! That's why you're self-luminous

You've captured my heart and illuminated my mind's eye
Because you light up my night's sky and take me on a natural
high

You're so radiant that your lustrous light is blinding me
The pursuit of your love is the only place you're finding me

It's the purity of your heart which gives you light that's seen
near and far
And that's why I love you because you shine just Like A
Star...

"BEAUTIFUL SMILE"

I'm still in awe and I don't believe it
But I know it's real because I just seen it So I pinched myself
to know I didn't dream it
A smile so beautiful my mind couldn't perceive it...

I've gone a lifetime and seen face after face
I've seen many smiles place after place
I've seen many emotions in various states
But your smile is the only one to make my heart speed up it's
pace...

I knew from the moment I first seen your smile That I would
never again have a reason to frown I'd never again have a
reason to feel down
And I'd have to show the world this beautiful smile that I've
found...

What comes to mind is Remarkable, NO!!, Spectacular to
my eyes

Your smile fills me with wonder and surprise
So ravishing, so astonishing, for your smile my heart cries
Your smile is so beautiful no words do it justice - I tell you no lies...

Your Angelic smile has flooded me with emotions, shaken me and left me numb
I'm lost in your rapture...Heaven has come...

I hope you don't mind but I can't help but stare
Because even when I close my eyes your smile is still there
And when you smile at me I wonder if you truly care
Because life without your smile is more than I could ever bear...

They say beauty's only skin deep, but when I look at you now
The only word that comes to my mind is "WOW!!!"
I must keep a smile on your face some way some how
Because more precious than gold is your Beautiful Smile...

"HOW MUCH I CARE"

All my life I've searched to find Thee
And I left Pain far behind me
Now your love is all I see
And to hold you in my arms is my destiny
That's where you belong - Where you're meant to be
Because I was locked out of heaven, but you love is the key
I'm intrigued by your lovely face, but it' s your heart that's the mystery
I have shared all I am with you and I hope you'll do the same eventually...

You're so lovely, but it seems that you're unaware
That life without you was more than I could bear And I didn't know what LOVE was until you came near
Now my life has light because you're here
Experiencing your love is pure ecstasy - Yeah you take me there
It's the ultimate Joy, and nothing else can compare

You' re a one of a kind beauty and that's why I stare
It only takes a second to say I love you , but a life time to
show you How Much I Care...

"JUST SCREWED"

I've traveled down Life's Highway searching to find
A way to live that gives my heart peace of mind
I'm left with no where to turn and no where to go
Scared that True Love is something that I'll never know
And these tears just keep falling down - I'm on my knees
balling
And the reason I'm stalling - Is because I hear "Death' calling
And I tried to be positive, but it's not working
You don't know the pain I feel inside - My hearts is hurting
And I don't know where to turn or what to do
I guess in life I'm Just Screwed...

Sometimes when it rains it seems to me the sky is crying
Because we pollute the world and the Earth is slowly dying
And the reality is that we did this to ourself
So in the end we can't blame anyone else
We've destroyed the planet in the name of "Mass Production"
And we're to blind to see in the end we'll end up with nothin'

There's still a chance to save the world and make things right
Because if we don't the world won't be able to continue to
maintain Life
So where can we turn or what can we do
Because without The Earth we're all Just Screwed...

"UNWORTHY"

Passion's fire keeps on burning
Time's ticking - The world keeps on turning Confusion
abounds without a guide's discerning Mistakes are made but
from them I keep on learning...

I have plans, so I make humble supplication to the One in
the sky
But what am I to do now that my plans have gone awry
I keep fighting because I don't want my dreams to die
But when your heart's broken it's hard to walk with your
head held up high...

Now with every second that pass
I wonder how long my life will last
Should I run from Death and dash
Or should I sell my soul for cash???

But for now I just rebuke those demons Sometimes I wish my

Pop's held on to his semen Perhaps this situation in life I wouldn't be in
They say we're gonna see Heaven, but for me it's hard to believe in...

Because my days are filled with struggle and strife Betrayal cuts like the sharpest of knifes
All I wanted was a house, kids and a wife
But Hell is where you dwell when Satan takes over your life...

What lives in the heart of men - Are we all bloodthirsty
Why is it so hard to admit I was wrong - Why does it hurt me
If repentance is a healer, reconciler and ends in mercy
Than why after the fact I still feel so Unworthy???

"THE DRUG LIFE"

Ain't this a Bitch!!!
How did my life come to this???
Shooting up, smoking, and drinking up what amounts to piss
Now only GOD can help you, because "Addiction" has the
firmest of all grips

I've nick-named you "Lefty" because ain't nothing about you
right
You've blown up more lives than T--N-T and dynamite
You dull a persons senses in thought, touch, taste and sight
And you destroy a person from the inside out once they let
you in their life

How could something so worthless be so addictive
How could people tolerate this poison and be so permissive
They would see that you're good for nothing if they were
more attentive
And everyone except the addict can see that this is no way
to live

Whether it's injected, a pipe hit, or another drink The one
doing it never stops to think
That their life could really be on the brink
Of turning into something that really stinks

Then it seems right before our eyes
You turn into something we no longer recognize
You keep saying that you quit but we all know you lied
Because every time we see you you're just so drunk and high
Your bloodshot eyes tell a very sad story
About a troubled life, about a life so stormy
I offered to help you change your ways so you could return to
glory
By paying for your rehab, but I was rebuffed when you
would ignore me

Now you're living in the ally-way - Begging for change -
People treat you like you're nothing You're eyes are bloodshot
red - You're hearing voices in your head - Telling you to do
something You've got holes in your shoes - Your breath stank
- Man your body's humming
You're the neighborhood bum and kids throw rocks at you
and get to running

Until one cold Winter night they find your body outside
And the ugliness of this here no one could ever hide
With slit wrist self-Inflicted from an old rusty pocket knife
All people could say is, "We've loss another one to THE
DRUG LIFE..."

"WHAT WOULD I DO WITHOUT YOU"

What would I do without all your inspiration
What would I do without your long-suffering patience

What would I do without you showing me how love's
supposed to be
What would I do without you being here to support me

What would I do without you gracing me with your smile
What would I do without you going with me the extra mile

What would I do without you fulfilling my every dream
What would I do without you leading our team

What would I do without you guiding my way
What would I do without you answering the prayers I pray

What would I do without you helping me to see clearly
What would I do without you to listen and really hear me

What would I do without you - My heart would be torn
What would I do without you- I'd wish I'd never been born

What would I do without you -I think I'd lose my mind
What would I do without you- Life's luster would lose it's
shine

What would I do without you- Life would be one big
sad song
Because without you...I'd have no one to call my own...

"THE EFFECTS OF TRUE LOVE"

You elevate me straight to the top
You've got curves on your body that just won't stop...

When we make love I don't ever wanna quit
I'll kiss you on your hips, thighs and your lips...

Whenever it's just me and you
There's so many things that we can do...

So many avenues to pursue
With our bodies stuck together just like glue...

The look in your eyes has me so excited
The way you're moving your body is so erotic...

When you leave my presence it pierces me like a knife
I swear I've never felt like this in my entire life...

Being wrapped in your arms is the ultimate pleasure

The love that I have for you can never fully be measured...

You satisfy all my senses that's why I feel so lucky And it's total gratification every time you touch me...

You're amazing, but it's your beautiful heart that's the ultimate stimuli
There's no greater joy than the love shared between you and I...

Every day with you is Christmas, and every night the 4th of July You're like a little piece of Heaven that's been taken from the sky...

I can't thank GOD enough, because you're the perfect creation of His Many search and never find, but now I know what True Love is...

"ALL THAT REMAINS"

Even if all is loss
I'll pay any cost
To be where you are
No matter how far
Because you've seen me at my worst, but I wonder why it is
That you could still love me even after all I did
And even through all the suffering and the shame My love
for you is all that remains...

Sometimes when it rains I wonder is the sky crying Why are
people's hearts so cold...Is "LOVE" dying???
Everyone is searching for love, but she seems to be hiding
Does GOD really love us or was that Preacher Lying???
So I sit in silence, but inside I'm sighing
Wishing people could see their true beauty, then there would
be no denying
That love is real , and I have you to thank without blame
Because my love for you is all that remains...

I know I'll never be the same
But even through the sorrow and the pain
And even though I'm locked up with these chains And even
though I's stuck in the rain
And even if they call me insane
In the end my love for you is ALL THAT REMAINS...

"BEAUTIFUL LOVE"

My heart...It beats for you
No one can do what you do

And when it seems I've loss my way
You're always there to rescue me

With a face oh so surreal
When our eyes first met our destiny was sealed

You've showed me how love is supposed to feel Our love is
something that no one could kill

"LOVE"... It's m ore precious than platinum - Stronger than
steel The purest of all qualities - The realist of the real

And I've found in you the greatest of all treasures
A love that stands the test of time - Eternally - Forever

And even if you tried you couldn't hide it Love just exudes from you - You can't deny it

That' s why my heart is set on you - I've already decided Because a love like yours is so rare that you have to hold on to It once you find it

You' re the only one to take my broken heart and mend it And when GOD was in the process of creation I know you are the product that He intended

Every time I needed a helping hand you were there to lend it And at the first moment I felt your love all of my sorrows ended

For the first time in my life I found something TRULY BEAUTIFUL
But you' re so humble that you didn't realize that you were beautiful

How anyone could deny you is beyond incredible Because you' re Perfection Incarnated and Infinitely Beautiful...

"OUR ONLY HOPE"

I'm trying to make it up to Heaven one day
That's why I always read Your Word and never cease to pray
So I've turned over a new leaf and changed my sinful way
Hoping You hear my prayers and the sincerity of what I say...

They say to make it you've got to believe and repent
So I believe and repent hoping GOD sees how much time I've
spent on my knees so long that my reality's bent
Because I know my soul's priceless, beyond dollars & cents...

So when my numbers called I hope that I'm ready
Because the specter of Death weighs on my mind so heavy
And at the crossroads of Heaven & Hell - Who'll meet me???
I hope it's my Savior and I make it into Heaven - If He let's
me...

It weighs heavy on my mind because nothing seems certain
Except Life & Death, Right & wrong, What feels good and
what's hurtin'

So pick your poison behind number one or two curtain
Because in the end it's either GOD or the Devil that you're
servin'...

And that's the realist thing I ever wrote
And that's the truest thing I ever spoke
Because in a world filled with the Devil's deceitful smoke
GOD's Love is REALLY our only hope...OUR ONLY HOPE!!!

"TO PROVE MY LOVE FOR YOU"

To prove my love for you...What should I do???
Should I get on my knees and give a ring to you
Should I climb the highest mountain and scream your name
Should I fight a lion and with a bear do the same Should I
cook you dinner and do the dishes
Should I be like a Genie and grant all your wishes Should I
work my fingers to the bone
Should I buy you a fancy car and a mansion for a home
Because I've searched for you for oh so long
And I know you're tired of being alone
I'm so lost in love, but it's brought me to you
So now tell me what I've got to do...To Prove My Love For
You???

To prove my love for you...What should I do??? Give you the
world and The Heavens too
Would mere affection be enough
How about knowing I'll always be there even when times get
tough

Should I open doors and pull out chairs
Should I rub your back and brush your hair
Should I buy you jewels and a diamond ring
Should I write you a special song that only we could sing I
want to say I love you in so many ways
And let you bask in my love like the sun's rays
I'm so lost in love, but it's brought me to you
And I'll do whatever I've got to do...To Prove My Love For
You...

To Prove My Love For You...I'LL DO ANYTHING!!!
Because without you sorrow is what life brings
So in you I've given my all
In hopes that one day you too would fall In love with me like
I'm in love with Thee
Because only your love can heal the broken heart that's
within me
That's why I tell you that you're beautiful
But you didn't even know that you were beautiful
That's why I'm here to show
That I love you and won't ever let you go
Now I'm so lost in love, but it's brought me to you Need I say
or do more..To Prove My Love For You...

"LOVE REMAINS"

Oh how I long
To sing you a special song
In my arms is where you belong Until all your sorrows are
gone...

Only time will tell
How you truly feel
And if this love is real
But with a kiss our love is sealed...

I just wanna be alone with you
And do what lover's do
My heart beats for only you I just wish you knew...

And I'm not lying
These are tears of joy that I'm crying
Because you're beautiful and there's no denying That my love
for you is undying...

In love there's no Fear or Pain
I love you through the sunshine and rain
Without "LOVE" the world would go insane
And even if I loss everything my love for you would still
remain...

"NEVER HEAL"

My heart will never heal
The pain that I feel
I is so unreal
But I know it's real!! I KNOW IT'S REAL!!!

And it's so cold
The way that Love goes
It make you lose all control
And that's why the tears always flow...

How could so much joy end in so much pain
How could the sun be out but it still feel like rain So I rack
my brain, but it's left me insane
How could I love you so much but you don't feel the same???

So now I sit alone to wallow
In all my grief and sorrow
Wishing that I could borrow
The will to face tomorrow...

I just wish you knew what you ment to me
Or that I could change my painful reality
Because a beauty like yours is rare to find or ever see
And the loss of your love has forever altered my destiny...

And this is so unreal
But I know it's real!! I KNOW IT'S REAL!!!
And with this pain I feel
I just know my heart will never heal...

"SHATTERED INNOCENCE"

At first it's a pat on the neck, then a pat on the butt Then the next thing you know you're being sexually touched
He waits until you're alone to do this, that and such
He bribes you with candy and pizza for lunch

He tells you you're special and you want to believe it
He says tell no one...This is our little secret
You're just a little kid so his con you received it
And you know somethings wrong, but you're too young to fully perceive it

Now he's doing things to hurt you further
So you say you're going to tell but he then he threatens to hurt your mother
You want him to stop, but you don't want him to hurt her
So now you're caught in the web of this deviants torture

At first you were a vivacious-happy-playful child But now you're acting out and you never smile Your grades are dropping and you're fighting now And this has been going on for quite a while

So at a parent-teacher conference they ask you what's wrong
But you're too scared to tell them what's going on
Because up until now you've held this shame and pain alone
And just thinking about it sends chills down your bones

Broken down, you tell them about the man who's been touching you every since
You were 4 years old, and how his threats brought you to a point of hesitance
And for OH SO LONG you've prayed for GOD's deliverance
From this perverted devil who's left you in a state of SHATTERED INNOCENCE...

"NO LONGER THERE"

Compared to my life, Hell would seem like paradise
The only man to suffer more than me was Jesus Christ
I try to believe but it's so hard for me
Because my world's so dark and pain is all I see
It seems like Tragedy is around every corner
When all hope is gone does that mean I'm a goner My life is
filled with Agony and Catastrophe
And ain't no one willing to come to Hell after me
I live my life in the clutches of a lion
Why every man that tries to change the world ends up
dying???
I mean look at The Messiah, Martin Luther King Jr. and
"J.F.K."
To change the world they had to die in the worst way
Now I'm at the point to where I just don't care
Because everything that I used to love ain't no longer there...

The "Heart" is so cold...WHO COULD EVER KNOW IT???

Wrath brings Death...If you don't control it I've fallen so
far...How much lower can I go
I asked GOD to tell me, but He didn't even know Because
there's no middle ground, everything's extreme
I've loss everything because the Devil picked my team
I had big dreams, but now it's a nightmare
And when you see a big butt and a smile...BEWARE!!!
Many Great Men have fallen victim to an evil woman
But the sway of the Devil is so treacherously cunnin'
We have all loved and lost which is so unfair
And most have to face life so unprepared
Now I'm at the point to where I just don't care
Because everything that I used to love ain't no longer there...

I've loss my grip on reality...
I've gone insane I can't escape this pain, not even with
Novacane
I rack my brain, but no answers do I find
Oblivion would be Bliss compared to this world so unkind
Sometimes I wonder...Did GOD really understand
What would happen when He created man
Do you really have to suffer to be declares righteous??
And if' we're all sinners does GOD even like us???
With sin comes shame and no place to hide
Scared when His Kingdom comes I'll be left outside
I can't front and pretend that I've done no wrong
I want to go back, but you can't get time back once it's gone
But now I'm at the point to where I just don't care
Because everything that I used to love ain't NO LONGER
THERE!!!

"MY BEST FRIEND"

You're my shoulder to cry on, and you calm me with your voice's soft tone
You've been more than a friend...You've been my backbone
Always there to take my calls on the telephone
It comforts my heart to know that I'm not alone...

Everyday I'm thankful that we have each other With a love deeper than a child and mother
And over time I've come to discover
That you're my one TRUE LOVE even though we're not lovers...

Your smile is absolutely Heaven sent
And your cool attitude is evident
The love we share is prevalent
I've found every aspect of you to be excellent...

I love the way you have my back You always make sure I never lack

You make me smile...You have that knack
You're pure JOY in human form...I applaud you with a clap...

You're magnificent...Absolutely perfectly created And over
time my love for you has never faded
They say no one's perfect, but since I've found you I can
debate it
You're wonderful!!! And anyone who met you would have to
say it...

Uncanny...Knowing you has made me a better man
You always cheer me up and lent me your helping hand
So from the bottom of my heart I hope you'll understand
That I Love You Without A Limit!!! You Truly Are by Best
Friend...

"ALL I NEED TO GET HIGH"

Your love is all I need to get high
Higher than the stars way up in the sky
Because without you all I did was just cry
And all my pain just seemed to multiply
Your love takes me high in so many ways
No more sad nights and no more lonely days
And I can see clear, your love took away the haze
But at the same time your love has me in a daze
When times got tough you stuck with me unfazed
That's why when I think of you I'm just so amazed
And I want you to know that I love you for sure
Your love gives me wings so that I can soar
Beyond the sky all the way up to Heaven's Door
Because a love like your's is what I've always searched for
And now I've found the answer to all of my prayers
Someone to love and someone who really cares
Who has my back and will always be there
Your love's got me high but you're still unaware
Of how much I care - Of how much you mean to me

You've got my head in the clouds - Higher than anyone
can see
It feels so great to have you just believe in me
They say "LOVE" is blind, but with us anyone can see
That we were meant to be, this is our destiny
Your love is the greatest thing in all of history
Your love's the greatest creation so I wrote about it on paper
If I could breathe in your burning love I'd get high off it's
vapors
Love is so exquisite - I give props to it's creators
All I need is your love - Forget the world and all it's haters
And as long as you love me, up to the sky is where I'll fly
Because Your Love Is All I Need To Get High!!!

"A MOTHER'S LOVE"

As boundless as the restless sea
As timeless as eternity
As endless as the stars above
To all who know it This is a Mother's Love

Mom
You have blessed me with this life and a strong will for living
You always bring out the love in me with joy peace and
giving
This is a Mother's Love

You have given me a mind to be loving caring and strong
Even though you always seem to be there to help me along
This is a Mother's Love

So many things about you Mom have always made me happy
that you are the biggest part of my life
And my love for you only grows as the years go by - by day
& night

You're a very special person compared to no other
And I am so very blessed to have you for my mother

So because you're thought about more than you could ever
know This comes to you on your birthday to specially tell
you so

HAPPY BIRTHDAY MOM!!!

"CONFUSION"

Where did GOD come from???
There seems to be some confusion
Is the life we live really just an illusion

A misconception of radical thoughts
Are our greatest accomplishments nothing but filthy rags to
be mocked

Is life just a meaningless hallucination
Or is there a greater purpose to our manifestation

I can see the purpose of sunshine and rain
But I struggle to see the purpose of disease and pain

We are all given life, but why it's taken away I can't see
I wonder if anyone else out there is feeling me???

For oh so long I've been drowning in sorrow and drowning
in fear

And I've prayed for answers, but things are still left unclear

Why can't things be plain and simple, black or white
Why is the Creator hidden from our sight

Is it because we as men pervert everything
You give us Why was the Messiah's death the only way to
forgive us

I just wish it could be You and me, for all eternity Like You
intended it to be...Can anyone see???

All these unanswered questions have left on my heart a deep
contusion Hoping on "Judgment Day" it will end all of my
Confusion...

"MY BROTHER FROM ANOTHER MOTHER"

Every time I see your smile
All I can say is "WOW!!"

And the times that I'm feeling blue
Are turned to joy when I think of you

You have such a positive spirit
That all are blessed when they come near it

You stay true in good times and bad
And your love took away all the pain I had

When I poured out my heart you really listen to me
And took away my despair with the love that comes from
only Thee

You always laugh at my dirty jokes
And you lift my spirits with the kind words that you spoke

You're in my heart and on my mind constantly Seeing your smile is my greatest joy...Honestly

Your my truest friend and our love runs deeper than all others
So don't let our love end, My Brother From Another Mother...

"LOVE...OH LOVE"

LOVE...OH LOVE...
Sometimes it makes you smile
Sometimes it make you cry
Most are left wondering why...OH WHY!!!

LOVE...OH LOVE...
Sometimes you've brought me joy
Sometimes you've brought me pain
A mixture of sunshine and rain...Ying-Yang...

LOVE...OH LOVE...
Your light will always shine
Even at nighttime
You mesmerize my mind...You're Divine...

LOVE...OH LOVE...
We deeper than husband and wife
I'll stand up for you and fight
You mean more to me than life...

For You I'll Sacrifice...

LOVE...OH LOVE...
In the depths of my troubles you helped me rise above
And flew me up to Heaven on wings of a dove
You're what dreams are made of...LOVE...OH LOVE!!!

"ALL IN A DAYS WORK"

As a doctor I knew I had to act quick
But I had none of my medical tools...OH SH*T!!!
I guess I'm gonna have to "Macguyver" it
Because I'm on the street with very little to work with...

I yelled for someone to dial "911"...PLEASE!!! Then I tried to
help the first man as he bleeds
I see it's not a serious wound but he's not fully out of the
weeds
In tears the man blurts out,"It's all my fault!!!", and for
forgiveness he pleads...

The first man's okay for now so I move to the second man
He's in much worse shape...ALL DAMN!!!
Stabbed in the stomach...He's really leaking
But I've got to keep him alive is what my mind keeps
repeating...

I take off my shirt and to the wound I apply pressure

Just then the second man says,"A brother's bond should never be severed."
I'm thinking he's going into shock or whatever
So I tell him to stay strong, you can make it, hold it together!!!

Then I looked at his face
I had to do a double take
There must be some mistake
I see the 2 men are identical twins...How did they come to this fate???

Just then the ambulance shows up and I tell them that
He's going Into shock so he needs 2 CC's of Ephinedrine STAT!!!
The knife went straight through his stomach and out his back
And if he's gonna make it you can't let his blood-pressure slack...

Both brothers made it but here's the dirt
The second brother's wife cheated on him with the first
I hope In the end they see that JEALOUSY & REVENGE leaves everybody injured and hurt
Because next time a doctor might not be around, but for me it's ALL IN A DAYS WORK...

"LIGHT & LOVE"

Darkness tries to cover and hide the evil inside While Light
exposes all whether truth or lies
Hate is unforgiveness...In the end everyone dies
Love is forgiveness...
Your life is precious in Her eyes

With Light & Love together on a united front
We'll show Darkness & Hate that we ain't no punk
As our Light overtakes their Darkness exposing their dirt
and junk
They scatter like water bugs...True to form they're chumps

Our bond is closer than a hand and glove
Search but you'll find none are Hood enough
To the joy we bring reigning from above
We Are Light & Love...

"TOGETHER WE'RE STRONG"

Please don't cry but if so let it he known
I'll kiss your tears away until they're all gone Because when
you cry you don't have to cry alone I'll cry with you...To-
gether We're Strong...

I lit 2 candles on a mountain at midnight
To show this dark world that we are each others light

When life's storms get rough I won't run and hide
No matter how tough life gets I'll never leave your side

Where others failed, gave up and left you hurt
I'll help you prevail and lift you up so our love can work

I'll always be there to wipe the tears from your eyes
But now they're tears from the joy we have in our lives

So when you cry let it be known

I'll kiss your tears away until they're all gone
Never again will you ever have to cry alone
I'll cry with you...TOGETHER WE'RE STRONG...

"YOUR SMILE"

I can no longer front or pretend
That I understand or comprehend
The beauty that lies within
Your Smile...

No need to be coy
All sadness you've made void
All who see it have joy
Your Smile...

You took my frown
And turned it up-side-down
Like rain to my heart's parched ground
Your Smile...

It's the absence of all pain
With JOY & BLISS that can't be contained
And leaves me with feelings that I can't explain Your Smile...

It's the key to Heaven's Door
The key to everything I'm looking for
But at the same time so much more
Your Smile...

I've traveled mile after mile
I've seen smile after smile
But none leaves me in AWE and saying "WOW!!!"
Quite like YOUR SMILE...

"THE GREATEST THING IN MY LIFE"

Your Love's a dime of all dimes
Which continuously blows my mind
Because like fine wine
It only gets better with time...

When you're around I could never feel blue
You fill me with a Bliss I never knew
So there's nothing that I'd rather do
Than spend all my time with you...

And where sorrow took root you should know
Your Love came in and made Joy grow
Seeds of Happiness is what you sow
You hold my heart in your hands...PLEASE NEVER LET IT
GO...

I feel so blessed to be
At one with you in unity
And every since you came to me

I've been living in Perfect Harmony...

You have a special way
To always brighten my day
As I keep tears of Joy at bay
"I LOVE YOU!!!" is all I want to say...

Loving you is easy to do
Because you're beautiful...I thought you knew
So please believe what I say is true
THE GREATEST THING IN MY LIFE IS **YOU!!!**

RAP SONG: "KING KONG"

(Verse #1)

I'm King Kong, I'm the one they waitin' on

For me to come - ring the alarm - I am the bomb

The Shogun - I show guns and niggas run

Quick to light a nigga up faster than the fuckin' sun

Call me "Gorilla", on the forrilla, a ill nigga

Bringin' pain to Yo person, the product of my trigga

I spit flame from my gat or a sipher

Make you sh*t Yo pants like a baby sh*ts a diaper

Giving heart attacks - This ain't fiction I'm speakin' facts

Knockin' heads off shoulders wit my fist and baseball bats

I done lost my mind - I think I was born to commit crime

A schizophrenic nigga that ain't scared to do time

So bring the bloodbath to my domain or my section

And I'll f*ck Yo ass up like a damn staph infection

So bring it on - Ring the muthaf*ckin' alarm

And sing my song, Muthaf*cka I'm King Kong!!!

(HOOK)

(Verse #2)

I'm King Kong, recognize game in Yo face

Life's twist-tee tied like a damn shoe lace

Put you in your place like a roach in the projects

You've seen a lot of niggas - ain't seen none like me yet

A rap phenomenal human being to the extreme

Straight out the guttah with hood rats and dope fiends Break you off a piece of crack - My rhyme's dope

Leave Yo head spinin' like some hunit spokes

Make a b*tch deep throat but don't choke

Off this King Kong Ding Dong down Yo throat

Because I'm a beast in the sheets while in between Yo cheeks I unleash MASS skeets, have Yo pussy sore fo' weeks

So get ready- get ready, because here comes the thrilla

"Vannessa Del Rio" tried to handle this dick nigga She said bring it on, so I carried it in my arms

Even Vannessa had to say..."**GOT DAMN, YOU'RE KING KONG!!!**"

(HOOK)

(KING KONG - CONTINUED)

(Verse #3)

I'm King Kong, bounce thru the hood like ping pong Quick to get in Yo a** like G-strings or them thongs You can run away but I'm still gonna blast Ya

You're pretty fast but my slugs they move faster They gone grab Ya - You gotta pay the penalty

I'm King Kong, you F*cked up crossin' me

So read these Nikes, as I stomp you on the pavement

And I hope your family can make your funeral arrangement

You done F*cked up and tried to steal from a "G"

Short for "Gorilla", King Kong, straight insanity

I gets bold, better yet I gets cold

To make sure my enemies don't live to get old

So free Yo mind before I end your sunshine

Prepare for Satan and eternal nighttime

So lets get it on, when I'm done you'll be gone

Don't ever F*ck with a gorilla like me. I'M KING KONG...

(HOOK)

HOOK :

I'M KING KONG, KING KONG, I'll KING KONG I'M KING KONG, KING KONG, I'M KING KONG I'M KING KONG, KING KONG, I'M KING KONG RING THE MUTHAF*CKIN' ALARM, PREPARE FOR THE STORM...

I'M KING KONG, KING KONG, I'M KING KONG I'M KING KONG, KING KONG, I'll KING KONG I'M KING KONG, KING KONG, I'M KING KONG I BLOW UP LIKE THE BOMB, LEAVE YOU HANGIN' LIKE "SADDAM"...

ACORSTIC POEM: "DREAMING'.

Dreaming of you always
Rejuvenates my spirit
Every time I envision you
All I feel is total elation
Making me want you more and more
Imagining a life of bliss where there's
No more pain or sorrow because we're together
Growing stronger in love while dreaming forever

Contrast Poem: "Wisdom & Foolishness"

Wisdom is the path to success and all knowledge
But foolishness is the path to failure and all garbage
There's wisdom in humility and foolishness in pride
Take a look at each and you'll soon see what they provide
With wisdom there's no limit to what you can learn and
create
While foolishness refuses to learn from past mistakes

Wisdom is a Priceless Jewel
Foolishness is a Worthless Tool
Wisdom is GOD given Foolishness is Satan's prison
So break the chains of "Foolishness" and leave him forsaken
Because "Wisdom" holds the crown that none have taken

"YOU'RE BEAUTIFUL"

Looking at the skies
I can see your eyes
And their beautiful
That can't be denied

Whether caterpillar
Or butterfly
Either way you're beautiful
In my eyes

You're the truth
In you there is no lie
And you're so beautiful
I could cry

My Angel from Heaven
You lift me up to fly
YES!!! You're beautiful
You take me high

You're Life itself
The reason that I try
Because you're beautiful
My only reason why

Where my heart was polluted
Your Love detoxified
You know you're beautiful
You saved my life

Though Greed & Pride ugly the world
You came to beautify
OH YOU'RE BEAUTIFUL!!!
You're Love's endless supply

Epilogue :

The true measure of Beauty-
is what I've seen in your heart, If I knew then what I
know now-
I definitely would have chosen you from the start...

You're the essence of LOVE-
only from you can JOY flow,
That's why I'll never let you go-
Because You're Beautiful!!!

"HOLDING ON TO EMPTINESS"

I can't believe I let You inside

Unforgiveness with all it's selfishness & pride

And I held on to You for dear life

But deep down inside I knew this wasn't right

My whole life I've been hurt and done wrong

So unforgiveness took root and I couldn't move on Really thinking I needed You but as time went by

You brought bitterness to my bones and made my spirit die

You stole joy from my heart until all my love was gone

But I clung to unforgiveness and still held on

I didn't know my eye for an eye attitude was a crime Because an eye for an eye in the end leaves everyone blind

And I was blinded by unforgiveness, holding on to old grudges

So I couldn't let go or heed The Holy Spirit's nudges

Locked in the prison of resentment every time it called

Not realizing I put myself behind these walls

In life you get what you give so I must forgive

Because holding on to unforgiveness is no way to live

Unforgivenes...I'll never be free with You inside of me

So I have to forgive in order to set my soul free Because I see You are worthlessness

And I have to let go of Unforgiveness

I have to let go of all it's bitterness I HAVE TO STOP HOLDING ON TO EMPTINESS!!!

   Epilogue:

The Scriptures say you have to forgive to be forgiven But for many "Unforgiveness" is an inescapable prison

We all be sinning and need to be forgiven

Because if given what we TRULY deserve none would he left living So let "LOVE & FORGIVENESS" be the forefront commencement Realize holding on to "UNfORGIVENESS" and it's bitterness YOU'RE JUST HOLDING ON TO EMPTINESS...

"YOU ARE THE ONE FOR ME"

Your sensuality is killing me - You blow my mind
Because every time I see your face the words are hard to find

Your lips and hips are shelter from the rain upon my kiss
I take your hand and my heart falls into total bliss

Longing for the warmth of your caress and your embrace
Every minute - hour - day...I'm thinking of your face

Because my heart it beats for you and no others
So lets lose ourselves in "LOVE" under the covers

What can I do to make this Love I feel a reality???
Look at my heart you'll see it's pure - YOU ARE THE ONE
FOR ME!!!

"MY NAME IS DEATH"

I'm deep. ..Deep like X-Rays
I bring terror like thunder, but still kill on sunny days
In many ways I engage all life with combat
But most are simple minded and afraid of my con tact
SCREW THAT!! I come with the ruckus or not at all
My Name Is Death, I'm coming for you, you hear my call
You run away, but one day I' ll make you pay
I'm here to stay so t here's no getting a way... I'm here to
slay!!!
Until there's none left, because in life there's no Ref
I'm a cold chef , because what I'm cooking is your death
Take your last breath, but why waste the energy
On my payroll I got the Devil working for me
He's cold too and we've got *a* deal that we do
It's about you!!! He gets your soul once I'm through
He sets you up and makes you want to squeeze that trigga
And when you do I applaud..."Death's" claimed another
nigga!!! My Name Is Death...

Who can you call when they all fail
You can count on me to have you as the walking dead inside
a prison cell I bring pain to those who fall into my traps
BEWARE, because I'm giving dirt naps
Did you know that I have a million way to get you My Name
Is Death and it's your life that I pursue You can fight, but I'm
going to win in the end Don't even try to pretend that you
don' t sin
Every minute we get closer to our destiny
And every minute you get closer to meeting me
The truth is tragic, because all who have battled me have loss
the fight
My Name Is Death *and* when I come nothing can save
your life
Once you' re gone people gonna sing them sad songs
Because I cut deep like tattoos or the marrow in your bones
All you can do is try to live your life right
Because you never know you just might meet "Death"
tonight...My Name Is Death...

I'm the one sure bet that you have in life
My Name Is Death and I' m cold...I kill on sight
I don't need *a* gang of niggaz with A-K's to bring it on
Because I can touch anybody and their life is instantly gone
With no get back, revenge or reprisals
And colder than the Arctic Winds with no rivals
My heart's blacker than a million moonless mid-nights
I bring fright, and the Devil's my homie...He sends me kites
With your name on it, I put your brain on it
To leave hole in your head... I bring pain - Want It???
I come in many forms, but none have found the answer
Kill you with guns, knives or take you out with Cancer
And I don' t discriminate between the weak and the strong

I'm the king killer that none can dethrone
I'm going to make your whole family sing them sad songs
And I won't be stopped until all life is gone...My Name Is
Death...

"YA SLIPP IN'"

This doctrine that I speak Is from GOD not man

Within GOD there's purity, but in man' s flesh there's sin

Who told you that it was cool to hate each other

Are we all sons of "Cain" because we kill our brothers???

Look deep into your heart... Do you know why you hate

Satan wants us all to die...Is this fact our fate???

How many souls have you save through The Blood of Christ??

Have you asked The Holy Spirit to engulf your life???

Are you tired of being tired Just to be tired again??

Accept Christ and He'll give you rest as well as forgive your sins

Why would any man choose to be lost and burn

6000 years of mistakes and yet we still haven't learned

Too head strong , we a ll wrong, none even try to he right

That' s why GOD put me here to bring you to the light

When people sin they think it's fun and they just might shoot ye

So If you sinning like the Devil GOD said to rebuke ya...YA SLIPPIN'!!!

So I rebuke ye and keep stepin' with Christ as my weapon

Even the Devil gets gone when I turn The Word on

And behind me I got The Army of Heavenly Host In my veins ice water, in my soul

The Holy Ghost GOD holds me close and He'll never let go

Just remember to tread slow because GOD said so And yet I still see a world full of Satan's spies

But I've been baptized In years of tears through GOD's patient eyes

A day spent wise is closer to Heaven than not

In the ghetto for every 1 to make it 7 more get shot

And eleven got hot an d chose the wrong path on the road

While the Devil laughs watching your destruction unfold

Do not pass go and leave your brother behind you

I got The Word on my tongue and I'm here to remind you

When you' re winning through sinning only the Devil is grinning

He's got you abusing an illusion, blind to your final ending...YA SLIPPIN'!!!

I'm here to tell you the truth, I got the plank out of my eye

To see clear to remove your speck then together we'll cry

Out to GOD for mercy because we used to hate and devour

And now we see GOD loves to rein down blessings and power

Upon your person with no rehearsing, but don' t flex with pride

Or you'll fall like the Devil who has no love inside

The Ten Commandments understand them, do you know GOD's rules???

You must repent, accept Christ and The Bible your tool

He's got the keys so get on your knees if you want to be freed

From this world with it's Lust, Pride, Wrath and Greed

Yes indeed, be slow to speak and quick to listen

Submit to GOD and come to Him before you make your decision

You got a choice to turn from sin and re-do your life

So let Him cleanse you from within then live for Christ

Or what you gonna say on Judgment Day when your sins unfold

Got caught slippin', died in sin and now you lost your soul... YA SLIPPIN'!!!

"MY QUEST FOR LOVE"

It seems my quest for love

has once again tried to take me under-

Where are you love

is what I used to always wonder -

Born in the ghetto slums

and treated like garbage since birth -

So love was scarce

in my life of low self-worth -

With no love from day one

I was born with a foot in my ass -

I feared the future because that foot has

remained from present and throughout all of my past -

When I saw the bright love of other families on T.V.

I longed for the light of that love to shine within me-

But my reality was bullets flying, brothers dying and hateful darkness as far as the eye could see-

I heard a wise man once said

"There's no failure in trying"...What's this all about???-

Because I'm all tried out...I'm all cried out "Love"...WHY DO YOU CONTINUE TO HIDE OUT??!!

In this world of woe

it's as if all the love is depleted or just gone-

But there's something deep inside that pushes me to keep carrying on -

Deep inside I know love is "REAL"

and don't ask me how...I JUST KNOW IT!!! -

The answer has always been deep inside of me I was just too scared to show it-

I was so foolish upon my quest

by looking for love in everyone else -

When all I had to do was look in the mirror

and my quest for love ended when I began to love myself -

Now I have a quest for all of mankind

to fulfill the "GOLDEN RULE" if only they could-

Which is to love others the way they love themselves

AND HOW AWESOME THIS WORLD CAN BE IF ONLY
THEY WOULD...

THE QUEST CONTINUES...

"I LOVE YOU MAMA"

June 28th, 1975
Was the date I was born still alive
Mama used to hold me In her arms, rock me to sleep
Kiss me good night and tuck me under clean sheets
Every time I would awake she would always be there
Hugging me and kissing me to show me that she cared
One day she taught me to tie my shoe, go to the potty too
Everything I knew she taught me how to do
I got to give Mama props for doing what she do
Once I tried to be sneaky, but she already knew I could never
pull a fast one on Mama
Neither could my sisters "Shirley", "Sonja" and " Latanya"
We was the average everyday "Hard-Head" kids
Mom whipped our butts for all the bad things that we did
Some call her " Tootsie", but now days it's "Flo-Joe"
Mama you're beautiful I just had to let you know...I LOVE
YOU MAMA!!!

Mama taught me to be a "Rida", growing up right beside her
4 kids at 19 with nobody to help guide her I never knew I put
so much stress on you
Stealing money out your purse and hanging with the
wrong crew
And Mama I'm so sorry for all the pain I caused
If I took heed to your advice I wouldn't be behind bars
Premonitions Mama gave I never thought would come true
But you were always right... I SHOULD HAVE LISTEN TO
YOU!!!
But I was young and dumb with a mind set to lose
Mama you're so strong that no one could ever walk in your
shoes
But ain't this a switch...Mama caught a case y'all
So stressed out... Drugs would be her down fall
I don't blame you Mama, you've been through Hell and back
Fighting Cancer, strokes, The Devil and Heart Attacks Some
call her " Tootsie", But now days it's "Flo-Joe"
Mama you're beautiful I just had to let you know...I **LOVE
YOU MAMA!!!**

Mama...You've always been there for me
Through my pain, countless tears and tragedies OH
MAMA!!! We deeper than the core of the Earth Our love
burns like lava that's about to burst
Me and my Mama...We like 2 peas in a pod
I thank you Mama for not spoiling me by sparing the rod
My dearest Mama knows how to make somethIn' out of
nothin'
If my life was In danger she would come out bustin'
And Mama you don't know what you mean to me You gave
me life, self-esteem and my identity **I LOVE YOU MAMA!!!**
Anything you ask I will do You used to watch over me now I
watch over you

No drama Mama...I' ll love you forever, that's right
I thank GOD for making you perfect and giving me life
Some call her " Tootsie", but now days It's "Flo-Joe"
Mama you're beautiful I just had to let you know…**I LOVE YOU MAMA!!!**

"MIND TRIPPIN'"

I woke up from a nightmare
To find that I'm living in a nightmare
I'm seeing things that are not there
And left wondering if GOD even cares

I'm seeing voices and hearing faces
I blackout and wake up in strange places
Where I'm naked and tied up with shoelaces Trapped in my
own mind with no way to escape this

Prayer at times seems to help
But terrors at night make my spirits melt
I'm "Mind Trippin'" alone with no one else
Trying to find a way to escape from myself

So I'm here to tell all who would listen
The mind is for some an inescapable prison
But it's also GOD's greatest gift and greatest mission
To renew our minds and keep us from "Mind Trippin'"...

"NO LOVE- (PART #1)

Your first love was nice to you so you fell real hard

You never thought he'd dog you out and leave you emotionally scarred

Dropping game he says you're special so won't you make love to me

So you fall deeper in love and lose your virginity Not knowing that he's already got 10 baby Mamas

And now you make number 11 because you fell for his drama

He got you pregnant, unprotected was his "JUHNSUN" in you

And now Mom and Dad want to know girl why did you screw

It was childish, you're just a child with a child on the way

And you love your baby daddy but that won't make him stay

He even kicked you in the stomach and said this ain't gonna work

And he left you brokenhearted and beat down in the dirt

Then he called you a slut and told you to net the hell out his house

Hurt beyond belief, you grab your clothes and you bounce

In fornication there's **NO LOVE** just the Devil's deeds

There's **NO LOVE** in sex out of wedlock just the Devil's seeds

No matter what the Devil offers it's not good enough

Because without GOD it leads to "Death" and a world of **NO LOVE...**

"NO LOVE - (PART #2)

You gave Tragedy, Pestilence and Pain

So when you meet your maker you gone get the same

Because you lived your life in "Flesh", you was proud to be a thug

So when you meet your Maker you won't get **NO LOVE**

Because in Heaven there are no Ghettos, GOD gives the Best

But you gets **NO LOVE** when you die in the sins of your "Flesh"

If you think I'm lying then you can put my words to the test

GOD gives you what you give so always give your Best

Because GOD can't stand sin, He must put it to rest

You showed **NO LOVE** in your life so you gets **NO LOVE** after death..(**FLAMES!!!**)

"THE GREATEST JOY TO ME"

I love you and there's no denying this feeling

Your presence refreshed my soul and brought spiritual healing

That's why moments with you mean more and more to me

Because the love of you brings the greatest joy to me And that love fills me thoroughly in height & depth

A love so powerful it conquers all in Life & Death

For bringing you into my life I thank The Father above Because you are an extension of His ever present love

Everywhere you go your love leaves it's mark

A mark that's been engraved at the center of my heart

So no matter the trial, tribulation or tragedy

No matter the pain, suffering or catastrophe

No matter what will come or whatever will be

I know your love will conquer all and be there with me I love you and there's no denying this feeling

Your presence refreshes my soul and brings spiritual healing

That's why moments with you mean more and more to me

Because the love of you brings the greatest joy to me...

"LOVE EVENTUALLY"

Love...How do I know you're real???
It's the feelings that I feel whenever you are near... Oh
Love...Where do we go from here???
It's the joy you bring that makes me sing and shed joyful
tears...
Oh Love...I'm so glad that you're in my life,
With the oneness that is shared between husband and wife...
Oh Love...What have you done to me?!!
No matter how hard you try you have to love Love
Eventually...

Love...Look how you've made me feel,
The pain in my heart is no longer there because you helped it
heal...
Oh Love...You've saved my wayward soul,
You bring peace and happiness when you are left in control...
Oh Love...I love you more everyday,
There's no sin in love only harmony when Love has it's way...
Oh Love...What have you done to me?!!

No matter how hard you try you have to love Love
Eventually...

Love...You're what everyone's looking for,
The personality of our Heavenly Father and what He has in
store...
Oh Love...How precious is your name???
There's purity in your passion and nothing vain...
Oh Love...In you there's nothing that I would change,
I would die for you, give the blood that flows through my
very veins...
Oh Love...What have you done to me?!!
No matter who you are you have to love Love Eventually...

"THINK TWICE"

LOVE...If you have to think twice maybe it wasn't ment to be

So I hope you don't have to think twice about loving me

When I first felt your love I was hesitant to accept it

But over time I found that your love never left me neglected

And sometimes all the wonderful things you've done for me slips my mind

But your smile reminds me of how your love transcends time

I can now say today

That we've come a long way

And where darkness used to be

The light of LOVE shines between you and me

The depths of my love for you is hard to explain

Because it's limitless love where only perfect bliss remains

Your spirit is the essence of LOVE - THAT'S A FACT So tell me you love me and I'll tell you back

It's hard to express how you make me feel inside

But I know you feel it every time you look into my eyes

This is the love of you that I'm feeling

Which has cleansed my soul and brought spiritual healing

Now all Pain & Sorrow has ended, Joy & Harmony are befriended

My broken heart is mended, all because your love is so splendid

LOVE...Think once, think twice is what some do

But I don't have to THINK TWICE to know that I love you...

"AT ONE WITH YOU"

Well I've been standing on my own two
But it's so lonely without you
So what am I gonna do???

And it don't matter whether near or far I need to be where
you are
Because you are my shining star...

I can see your smile when I close my eyes You're like a piece
of Heaven taken from the sky
And you take me there - Like a natural high...

No matter where I travel - No matter how far I go No matter
the sorrow - No matter how the tears flow
No matter where I end up...My heart will beat for you...

Loving you is my Greatest pleasure - My most joyful duty
Nothing could ever diminish your Absolute Beauty
But it's the inner beauty of your heart that always moves me...

You make my life bloom like Spring With so much joy I want
to sing
Your love does these type of things...

I love your laughter and your spirit, too
You've made me a better person and showed me what love
can do
So now my one life's mission is to be At One With You...

"YOU AIN'T NEVER HAD A FRIEND LIKE ME"

When your love was locked away I came to set it free
Your heart was the lock and my love was the key
Trust I'll never let you down, look into my heart and you'll
soon see
That You Ain't Never Had A Friend Like Me...

Others play games but I won't front or pretend Because I love
you deeper than most can comprehend
I'll be there from beginning to end
Whether you're righteous or sin Whether you lose or win
I won't break or bend
When all seems loss and LOVE is hard to apprehend
Your broken heart I'll mend
From all who contend
Your very life I'll defend
When you need it, my helping hand I'll extend
To lift, you up- Never again to descend
Other let you fall but I helped you ascend
Because I love you deeper than most can comprehend...

When your Love was locked away I came to set it free
Your heart was the lock and my love was the key
Trust I'll never let you down, look into my heart and you'll
soon see
That You Ain't Never Had A Friend Like Me…

Whether Good or Bad, Happy or Sad, Glad or Mad I'll always
be the best friend you ever had...

I wrote this so that you would know and believe That
nothing is greater than my Love for Thee...

Within the sphere of my love is where you'll always be
Because You Ain't Never Had A Friend Like Me!!!

"THE CROSS I MUST BEAR"

The loss of your Love is the cross I must bear
Because of my immaturity I never showed you that I cared
And I didn't appreciate you when you were here
So alone on this cross I weep bitter tears...

I paid you no attention...It's my fault that there's no longer us
I was out doing my own thing...You should have been my main focus
I did you so wrong that a billion apologies couldn't do you justice
The loss of your Love is an unbearable cross that's tortuous...

Being Selfish, Foolish & Clueless...I loss your Love When all you did was greet me with compliments and a hug
I was just disrespectful when push came to shove
So I bear a cross for not recognizing an Angel from above...

The Heaven of your smile has been gone for TOO long
Now Pain and Sorrow is my daily song

So I'm filled with Misery and Bitterness in my bones
Now Darkness is all I have - The Light of your Love is gone...

Confused and in the dark, I live in fear

The fear of never again having you near
WHY DID I PUSH YOU AWAY??!! It's my fault you're not here!!!
Now the loss of your LOVE is The Cross I Must Bear...

"A LITTLE BIT OF EVERYTHANG"

I'm day - I'm night
I'm wrong - I'm right
I'm darkness - I'm light
I'm blind - I'm sight
I calm hostilities - I argue & fight
I'm the lowest of low - I'm the greatest of height
I stand firm - I take flight
I'm weakened by sin...I repent to find might
I'm the agony of defeat - I'm victory proclaimed I'm a failure
that overcame
I'm The Ying & The Yang
I'm a little bit of everythang...

I'm the Abyss: - I'm a Higher Plane
I'm different - I'm the same
I'm heart attack serious - I'm a silly game
I heal - I maim
I'm off target - I have perfect aim
I accept responsibility - I dole out blame

I'm the coldness of ice - I'm the fire's flame
I'm a peacemaker...I'm War's wrath inflamed
I'm the agony of defeat - I'm victory proclaimed I'm a failure
that overcame
I'm The Ying & The Yang
I'm a little bit of everythang...

I'm pleasure - I'm pain
I'm sunshine - I'm rain
I'm of sound mind - I'm insane
I'm the righteousness of "Abel" - I'm the wickedness of "Cain"
I'm wild - I'm tame
I'm glory & pride -
I'm sin & shame
I'm beyond the norm - Yet I'm within The Creator's frame
I know I've come far...But I don't know why I came
I'm the agony of defeat - I'm victory proclaimed I'm a failure
that overcame
I'm The Ying & The Yang
I'm A Little Bit Of Everythang...

Epilogue:
Am I everything I was created to be???
Heavenly Father I just don't know...Only You can tell me
There's good and bad in everyone and in all
So forgiveness and mercy is all we can hope for when "Death"
calls
Just know the Father's Love for us will never change
So enjoy life, He's given us a little bit of everythang...

"PRAYER"

Behind prison walls I use prayer to cope I've found speaking to GOD fills me with hope

No matter how dark things seem in my life

Prayer always lifts me up into GOD's light

Prayer's vital to the communications

Between GOD and all of His creations but most are too prideful and impatient

To give GOD time so they just forsake Him

If' they knew His love and took time to pause

Through prayer we could break these chains-Break these walls... PRAYER...

"YOUR LOVE'S LIGHT WITHIN ME"

Living in such a cold world had me walking in the darkness
of Hate
Abused my whole life...I never thought your love would
change my fate

Until I met you I'd never really been loved
Only brokenhearted by Lust and holding a grudge

But you are everything I need and more
Far greater than anything I wanted or could ever ask for

The level of your love is infinitely higher than the rest
All because every aspect of you is better than the best

For you are the incarnation of Love's Perfection "GOD" made
you that way from your very inception

So I thank you for sharing yourself with me
For giving me hope and a real reason to still believe

But more than that, you've refreshed my soul from being
utterly bitter
And set my heart's passion aflame after being cold as Winter

You continue to surprise me with different aspects of Love
more and more
That's why I'm grateful to have you in my life to love and
adore

Once again I thank you for filling me in on how AWESOME
Love can be
And I no longer walk in Hate's darkness for your Love is The
Light Within Me

"WHAT YOU MEAN TO ME"

In your presence
is where I long to be-
The beauty of your smile
still amazes me -And in my dreams it's all I see -"Agape
Love" can't even express
what you mean to me...

Try as I may but
All my efforts were in vain-
Because the full scope of my love for you mere words can't
explain-
For it is a passion that burns
with an unquenchable flame-
But it runs so deep that
it can't be named or full proclaimed...

I want you to feel for me like I feel for you-
But for our hearts to beat as one Love has to be the glue-

So I've done everything in my power for that to happen
between us two -
For that is my greatest desire my greatest dream come true...

From the moment we first met
you've shown nothing but love for me-
I haven't been able to find the words to fully express my love
for Thee -
For there are no words in existence
that convey the depths our love entirely-
Because not even "Agape Love" can fully express
WHAT YOU MEAN TO ME!!!

"PAIN"

Sin & Death inter-wed and conceived a child named "PAIN"

Who grew up to bring suffering, agony & shame

All my efforts to escape Pain's chains -

Were futile and even in vain

I'm going thru pure Hell with the off-spring of "Cain"

I want to give up, yet I resist and strain

And I've come so far -

But now I wonder why I came

And though the pain is getting worse -

The Love in heart will still remain

Many allow their Love to falter under Pain's tyranny-

But my heart won't ever change

And though the pain is overwhelming at times-

The Love within my heart stays the same

And even though things are bad...Terrible even-

It's you "Pain" that I have to blame

Dealing with you and inner demons I've lost my mind -

And damn near gone insane

This Pain thing ain't no game-

It's made me cry so much people thought it had rained

Pain...I NEVER WANTED THIS THANG -

Because you stole my Joy and left my spirit maimed The lesson learned and knowledge gained-

Is not to allow you to destroy everything

I now know you were put here to keep the wild tame-

To keep us wise and using our brain

But what I find most strange -

Is there seems to be no Life, Love or Hope without Pain

And I've tried everything to escape Pain's Flames -

But "GOD" put you here for my spiritual growth to contain & maintain

So I still hold on to the Love that my heart contains-

For I've found that Love is the only antidote to counteract the venom of PAIN

In "GOD's" infinite wisdom He wanted us to experience everythang -

Which includes The Good & The Bad, The Ying & The Yang

But also Love & Hate, The Sunshine & The Rain -

The Greatest of Joy...And even the depths of PAIN...

"HOLDING ON TO EMPTINESS" (PART #2)

Another lonely night waiting on you -
But you're out in the streets
doin' what it do -

With patience & humility flowing thru my veins -
I waited for you
but you never came -

And to think you once told me that you'd love me forever -
But you had a wondering eye
so passion couldn't burn whenever we were together -

On my end I always came correct showing you loyalty and
full respect -
And in return what did I get
ASININE EXCUSES, LIES & BULLSH*T!!! -

Life with you was HELL
and everyday together I was reliving it -

But I held on to you not realizing that I was holding on to emptiness -

During the whole relationship I felt alone so many times I thought about leavin' -
But even though you were cheatin'
I still held on...WHAT WAS I THINKIN'??? -

But now that I have time to reflect now that I have time to recollect -
I'm glad I went thru that SH*T
because now I know who NOT to get involved with-

They say your best teacher was your last mistake but you know what I learned from all of this??? - Sometimes to be strong it's better to be alone AND STOP HOLDING ON TO EMPTINESS!!!

"COUNTING THE WAYS I LOVE YOU"

How do I love Thee??? Let me count the ways
It's hopeless, because I can't count them all within my lifetime
of days

And even in the span of infinite time
The number of ways I love you are beyond my finite mind

Because I love you in every way and on every level
And that's why you are my hope that I hold on to and I won't
ever let go

One, I love you - Two, I need you
All because you showed me "LOVE" when you didn't even
need to

Three - Four, You're the one I adore
On this side of creation no one could love you more

Five - Six, My glass heart had been shattered by bricks

Thought to be damaged beyond repair but your love brought a permanent fix

Seven - Eight, You took my low spirits to heights far and great You've brought back my joy and changed my fate

Nine - Ten, If loving you is wrong I don't wanna be right For I was e lost soul and your love saved my life

So how do I love Thee??? Let no count the ways
It's hopeless, because I can't even count them all within my lifetime of says

"ABOVE ALL OTHERS"

A child is a gift

form "GOD" to all mothers -

But a mother's love for her children is a blessing above all others-

I know first hand

because I feel that love everyday-

That's why my love for all mothers is deep far deeper than mere words could ever say-

A mother's love is the gift that keeps on giving -

For it is boundless, unwavering limitless and unending-

It's the source

of every family's strength -

And all the greatness of family it has you to thank-

And when I found myself in trouble you were there for me every time -

Giving me encouragement and hope with a stern hand yet still kind-

I can't count how many times you went without to make sure I never lacked-

And no matter how bad I'd been

you corrected me and still had my back -

YES I've made so many mistakes but you used them to teach me the most valuable of lessons-

As a youth I took you for granted

Not knowing you were my greatest of blessings-

That's why I'll forever love you with all of my might-

Realizing you are my greatest treasure the "Crown Jewel" of my life-

True indeed, a child is a gift from "GOD" to all mothers-

But mothers are "GOD's" greatest creation

A GIFT FAR ABOVE ALL OTHERS...

"HOW YOU MAKE ME FEEL"

Every time I see you there's a smile on your face
Which makes the sorrow in my heart fade until it's erased

But it's much more than your smile that soothes me
It's the beauty of your spirit that really moves me

You bring joy to everyone with your "Kooky" personality
But it's the beauty of your heart that keeps on attracting me

Because we are of a kindred spirit You and I
And our intertwined spirits create a love that won't ever die

You're the "Ying" to my "Yang" You're my everything
Bliss is what you bring to my life And you've made all my
wrongs right

I love all that you are and always will
It's because of who you are...That's How You Make Me Feel...

"WHAT REALLY MATTERS"

You never knew that I loved you
How can this be
Everything I do is for you
So why can't you see
That I love you so much
But apparently
You never had a hunch
About what you mean to me...

No romance without finance
I made sure our dollars were right
Now I see chasing those dollars ruined any chance Of us
having a relationship that would stay tight "Catch 22" - How
could I enhance
Both Love and Career for a future that's bright
It's a tangled web, a slippery slope, a dark delicate dance
I hope it's not too late for us to rekindle our Love's Light...

Honey I'm sorry for leaving you neglected

I got caught up in the "Rat Race" and the world's meaningless chatter
When you'd speak to me it should have been respected
All you wanted was me, but I was too busy climbing the "Corporate Ladder"
I didn't give you any time, love or make you feel protected
But from this day forward I now know what you're after
Everything you do or say I'll take to heart and fully respect it
And make sure you feel loved everyday...That's What Really Matters...

"A SAD DIFFERENCE"

At first you made me so glad Thinking it was "LOVE" that we had

I really believed we were solid...IRONCLAD

But as soon as times got tough and we hit a snag

You didn't even have my back and more stress is what you'd add

I always spoke to you kindly but you'd still go all "Nuclear Launchpad"

Then it'd go from bad to worse when you'd get mad

You'd lash out and use me as your personal punching bag

Why for all the good I'd give you in return you'd give me all bad

Why is a house with you no home and I feel like a "Nomad"

They say "LOVE" is a battlefield - A war like in "Baghdad"

But I want this war to end because I'm tried of being armor-clad

My LOVE you've left me in shambles...HOW COULD YOU DO ME SO BAD??!!

Because it wasn't LOVE but INFATUATION and the difference is tragic and so sad

"THE REAL LOVE WITHIN YOU"

I have been longing for Heaven but living in Hell
And the life I've lived was the ultimate cautionary tail
It's because of my Lust, Pride and Greed that from Grace I fell
But through it all your Love & Support never faltered or
failed

I was stuck in the fog- I was stuck in the rain
And rejected as something foul & profane
Most in my shoes would have gone insane
But thoughts of you help ease the pain

And as the pain multiplied
You helped stem the tide
And it's the love that you supplied
That really saved my life

Before you "REAL LOVE" is something I never knew
So I fell for "LUST" & "INFATUATION" and never had a clue

Of all the pain & destruction that that fantasy would do
But all that changed...Because of The Real Love Within You...

"COME BACK PLEASE"

A Homie

Long time no see

It's like you no longer know me

Life without you is so lonely

But the love in my heart is for you only

It's apparent to all so why can't you see

That we were meant to be

That we have a destiny

To be united as one eternally

But since you've been gone I'm locked outside without a key

To the gates of your love which was so Heavenly

Yet I still wait for you patiently

For you to make things the way they used to be

Because you're my Homie, my friend, my family Why did you go away??? Why can't you see???

That without you there is no me...

Come Back please...

"LOVE & FAMILY"

They say blood is thicker than water
But I say Love is what gives Family it's power

Love & Family...I live for you everyday
Your affections are priceless...How could I ever repay

Unspeakable are the utterances you've left deep within my
heart
So I'm left speechless and unable to live life when we're apart

For within you is an Indescribable radiance, absolute beauty
and Heaven brought near
You are a miracle of "GOD"... His way of letting me know
He's here

How you make me feel is hard to express within time &
space's limited frames
Now I understand that there are some emotions that have no
names

But Love & Family there's something about you - Something I never knew
Something pure & true - That's why I'm hooked on you

The full scope of my passion for you Is on full display for all to see
But most won't understand the depths of how much you mean to me

For through all my faults, rights & wrongs, pain & struggles you remained faithful
So if your face Is the last thing I get to see than I will be grateful

Because a family united Is a love that never stops caring
And Love is something that Family never stops sharing

For Love is the blood In my Veins helping me to carry on happily
But blood doesn't make Family... Love makes Family...WE ARE FAMILY!!!

ACKNOWLEDGMENTS

I want to give a very special thanks for the direct and indirect inspiration and influence for this poetry book being created to my Mother and Father (Flora "Tootsie" & Wayne "Bigg Weez"), Shirley, Rodney Sr., Jr., 3dr, 4th, & 5th, Natasha "Sexy Chocolate", and Phoenix "P", Nachole "Chicken", Cameron Sr., Cameron Jr. "C.J.", Nylah, Sonja, Jasmine, Dion, Latanya, Tanasha "Sha-Sha", Tiesha, Letrice, Lajoyce, Kurtis Sr., Kurtis Jr., my Grandma Catherine, Grandma Edith, Grandpa Clyde, Bill & Cookie, Jack M., Jack R., Sean, Cian, Elizabeth "Betsy", Maeve, Tony, Sara, Maddie, Ben, and The Cats "Tucker" & "Payton", Damean "CHAMP", Charlotte, Kareem "Mr. Kingstah", Inez, DRE, Buddy, Betty, Reggie, Issac, Keith, Pastor Clark, Pastor Carter, Linda K., Christine "Shuki", James "J.D.", Brianne, Rico, Corn, Eric, Cee-Cee, Kaoni, My long lost sisters Gloria & Sherekia, Anthony "Gold-Toes", Gomel "Strainj", Myasia, Jay R.I.P.), "BIG MIKE", Ronald, Melvin, Kip. Mis. Grove and the attorneys at "C.A.P.", "Pretty Tony", Pastor Tim, Pastor Sam, Rick J. Rick D., Access Ministries, Maya Angelo, Johna S., Grace C., Angie P., Dwell, Vannessa

L., Tyesha L., Elijah, Kesha, Sharita, Grandpa Russel, Poopie, Coolie, Daren, Jose & Jr., Riquita, Sierra, Aunt Marie, Uncle Walter, Uncle Vincent, Uncle Larry, Uncle Mark, Lashanda, Michael, James T., Jonathan, Joycelynn, Jermaine, Jeremy, Jaki, Jamilah, Ja'lynn, Joseph, Coach Bennett, The San Quentin Mental Health Program, ALL THE BROTHERS & SISTERS ON THE ROW, all the Poets/Spoken Word Artist/Rappers and Song Writers in the world. Please keep on doing what you're doing to inspire every new generation that are blessed to come into existence...I also want to shout out end give a special thanks to my spiritual brother "RU--AL" for giving me the blue prints to getting this poetry book published...Thank you my brother!!! I also want to thank everyone that chipped in to help fund the publication of this poetry book. Finally I want to thank You HEAVENLY FATHER FOR GRANTING ME YOUR MERCY, PERFECT UNDERSTANDING AND YOUR FORGIVENESS, AS WELL AS FOR NEVER GIVING UP ON ME...I LOVE YOU FATHER!!! And for anyone that I forgot to mention please forgive me I LOVE YOU TOO...

-PEACE 2 U ALL!!!-
LUH YA!!!

GREGORY "G-BONE" WHITESIDE JR.

Poet/Spoken Word Artist

I was blessed with life on June 28, 1975. I was the 4th and last to be born from my mother who was only a child herself; and at only 19 years old with 4 small children, no education and limited resources life was very rough for us all. I was the youngest of my siblings and also the only boy so I learned to respect women from an early age. I never got to know my biological father, but I did get the chance to see him briefly a few times every blue moon while growing up. I always wondered why he never made more of an effort to be in my life, but now I understand that he was dealing with his own physical, spiritual, and mental illnesses. Growing up with my young mother was tough. She was really too immature and inexperienced to be trying to raise us kids so yes she made many mistakes and because of the stress of it all she got involved with crazy men, drugs, and the street life of hustling to survive. Eventually all of her relationships ended badly and the drugs took over; so you can imagine what life was like for me and my sisters. We were constantly moving from place to place so it seemed like I was always the new kid at countless schools. The only good thing about that was by going to different schools every year was the kids at the new schools didn't know that I was wearing the same clothes year after year. Well for all of the stress and strain of life I still managed to do alright in school, avoid the pull of gangs & drugs and for the most part stay out of trouble. I played basketball and ran track for my high school teams (I actually went to the same high school for my last 3 years) and I graduated on time thanks to my Mom and Step Dad. The problem was after high school and a failed attempt at college, I had no plan or sense of direction as for what I wanted to do with my life. I had always liked to rap and listen to love songs so I bought some studio equipment and started rapping with the homies, but in the meantime I had to make a living so I took a bunch of dead-end jobs and after a while I saw that I wasn't happy with the direction and really slow pace that things in my life and career were moving. I became frustrated and ended up bumping heads with Mom's & Pop's at home and got put out the house. I then moved in with my sister

(Shirley) and found myself in a position to where I had to find a career path with the quickness. I ended up getting into Commercial truck driving. The plan was to gain my experience, save up money and eventually start my own trucking company; and I was still dabbling with producing rap music for my homies. The problems came in with the woman I was involved with which eventually led to me catching the case that brought me to Death Row. I'm not going to go into details about my case, but I would like to say that the legal system as it is today is not about justice...It's about Winning, Losing, and **MONEY!!!** No matter how innocent you are once you get involved in this **VERY CORRUPT SYSTEM (Unless you're rich) YOU ARE PRETTY MUCH SCREWED!!!** These prisons are filled with the mentally ill, Drug Addicts, the poor and some that are literally insane; most of which can be rehabilitated **if only given the chance.** I've been through some horrific things throughout my life and as a result I suffer from "P.T.S.D.", and I've found that writing poetry to express how and what I'm feeling helps me to get through the worst of times and that sharing my thoughts & emotions is a way to spin this horrifically negative ordeal into something positive. These poems are my outlet and lifeline whenever I need to release things that are on my heart whether they be Joy or pain, spiritual or worldly, good or bad...These are my most intimate thoughts & emotions which are a reflection of my inner soul and the depths of my heart. Well I hope as you go through the journey of the different layers, textures, and flavors of my poetry that they will touch your mind, body, and soul. From heartache to soul mates, from politics to religion, from simple to abstract; there's a little bit of everything in here to infuse you with my POETIC **SPIRITUAL EMBODIMENT**. As always I will continuously pray for my family, friends, all my fellow incarcerated brothers & sisters and for all of Humanity as a whole...And For all the courts that are handing out Death Sentences, here's some "Food For Thought": Though I'm on Death Row I'm walking in the same shoes as Yahshua ("Jesus"), The Apostles, the men-women-children or The Holocaust and the countless others who have been unjustly sentenced to "DEATH". In life you get what you give...THINK ABOUT THAT OKAY??? HATE, VIOLENCE, REVENGE, FOOLISHNESS, PRIDE, AND UNFORGIVENESS COME FROM THE DEVIL. WHILE LOVE, PEACE, MERCY, WISDOM, HUMILITY, AND FORGIVENESS COME FROM ELOHIM ("GOD")...WHICH WAY WILL YOU CHOOSE???

ALWAYS LOVE WITHOUT A LIMIT,
HUMBLY YOURS,
Gregory "G-BONE" Whiteside Jr.

9 781949 576221